THOUGHT LEADERS REACT TO
ANSWERING THE THREE CAREER QUESTIONS

"When it comes to our careers, most of us say we want answers, not questions, but the reality is that you have to ask the best questions before you can get the best answers! This book gives both in right order and in very thoughtful and insightful ways that make real sense."
—Dave Opton, Founder, ExecuNet.com

Bruce articulates laws of physics that rule an increasingly turbulent career universe. Answering The Three Career Questions is the new flight plan for anyone testing a personal business model.
—Tim Clark, author of *Business Model You*®

This book fills a huge gap in the literature. Having taught MBA and MS students now for five years I can attest to the huge need for a practical and analytical method to help people make choices in their careers. The amount of distress that occurs with the often messy career change paths can be greatly reduced by using this method which allows for looking at options in new ways. Bruce's level of expertise comes through in the writing of this book as does his compassion for the difficulty of making such choices. This is a real contribution to the many workers who wonder "which way shall I go next"—a much needed roadmap. Thank you.
—Lauretta Young, MD, Chief Emeritus Kaiser Mental Health, OHSU Instructor OHSU-PSU Health care MBA and MS programs

---

What I love about Bruce's approach is his focus on enduring questions and his commitment to career development as a relational activity more than a transactional one. He offers the reader lots of sage advice culled from over two decades of helping people successfully adapt and thrive in their work. The book is filled with great examples from actual clients to illustrate the key principles in his system. Bruce has a natural, thoughtful and pragmatic style as a writer and, as a result, the book is very approachable and useful.
—David Drake, editor of *The Philosophy and Practice of Coaching* and Founder of the Center for Narrative Coaching and Narrative Design Labs

◆

While written with the language of private enterprise, Mr. Hazen's insights are just as applicable for those who have chosen (temporarily or permanently) to work in the public sector. And it's particularly important now, when government work is changing just as radically as the private sector. The same 3 Questions apply universally.

What is universal is these specific questions, not their answers. But he doesn't leave us completely on our own with the questions. Copious examples and case studies take the reader through how these questions worked for others, and we learn from them, too.

Mr. Hazen's book is about how to get a career—not a job. I wish I could have read it 30 years ago.
—Chris Barns, Natural Resource Specialist with the U.S. Department of the Interior, Bureau of Land Management

◆

Answering The Three Career Questions is filled with so many insights and pearls of wisdom that it is truly a mind expanding experience to read and contemplate. From devices like the "Think Out Loud Laboratory" (TOLL) to his focus on time as "career fuel," Bruce dismantles the passive job-holding paradigm and teaches us to think of our careers as "controlled experiments" that can have intentional (and serendipitous) turns, ultimately leading us to a kind of steady state that he refers to as: "career self-reliance."

A wonderful and enlightening read.
—Don Grambsch, Senior Vice President for Corporate Development, Riverland Ag

Answering The Three Career Questions

Your Lifetime Career Management System

Bruce Blackstone Hazen

Three Questions Consulting
Portland, Oregon

Three Questions Consulting
Portland, Oregon
www.ThreeQuestionsConsulting.com

ISBN-13: 978-1489582140

Printed in the United States of America

CONTENTS

PART II:
USING THE THREE CAREER QUESTIONS

PART III:
SPECIAL SITUATIONS

Contents

ACKNOWLEDGMENTS

How Did this Happen?

One day, my good friend and fellow writer, David Drake, saw that his publisher was looking for experts to write the chapter on Career Coaching for the Sage Handbook of Coaching (2010). With one suggestion from him, and the advantage of a dream writing partner, Niki Steckler, I was offered a chance to write. I subsequently noticed that writing and being edited didn't leave any scars, bruises, or bad tattoos.

Now for the others that kept this momentum going—

To my blogging and career consulting colleagues who said to Tim Clark, author of *Business Model You* (2012), "You need to talk to Bruce Hazen about your book." Suddenly, I was a contributor to another book. Again, no scars or bruises, but a really cool tattoo this time.

To Brian O'Driscoll, Director of Career Services at Pacific University, who listened to me lament the difficulties of finding the right editor and one week later introduced me to Jocelyn Godfrey who got it done.

To David Kidd, my most enthusiastic Board Member at the Family Crisis Center. When I had just landed my most impressive job in the most impressive company of my career, he had the provocative wisdom to ask me, "What are you going to do next?"

And certainly to my thin, attractive and CPR-certified wife, Jennifer, who prevented this book from being published posthumously.

Last and not least, to my clients who offered me all their stories and showed me how their careers work and don't work well, I offer this Ode:

ODE TO MY CLIENTS
It's all owed
To my clients

QUICK PRE-TEST:

WHICH QUESTION MATTERS MOST TO YOU?

The Three Career Questions that frame your career management process over a lifetime are:

1. **When is it time to _Move Up_ in your profession or organization?** (This could mean progressing in your development, not just being promoted to a higher paying job.)
2. **When is it time to _Move Out_—when your profession, the work, your boss, or the organization are no longer a good fit?**
3. **When is it time to _Adapt Your Style_ for greater success?**

Up? Out? Adapt? Pretty simple. Compellingly simple! Something you can easily remember.

These Three Career Questions represent basic _career physics_ in the universe of your professional development. Our work lives, at least for most of us, have become complex—often due to forces and needs we may not even see or support, yet feel we must respond to or anticipate. Much like gravity, you don't have to like these forces (such as global economics, climate change, demographic shifts, and currency fluctuations), but you do have to respond to them. In an evolving, global work culture which is in perpetual and accelerating change, those individuals who understand the laws of career physics will be able to anticipate and control their own moves better than others who seem to just tumble with the forces around them.

Much of my career consulting work has involved helping clients consider different questions than the ones they originally came to me to answer. Becoming aware of all Three Career Questions, and the fundamental guiding quality they can represent, equips you to operate your own career GPS (geographic positioning system) and become more aware of where you are in your career at any given point.

Be aware that it's also possible to astutely answer, "Not now," to all Three Career Questions:

- **You may answer, "Not now," to <u>Moving Up?</u>** because you're working at the **right** level in the organization or at the right level of your personal development for this stage of your work or your current age.

- **You may answer, "Not now," to <u>Moving Out?</u>** because you're in work that is a **good** fit for you at this time, and you have a boss, organization, and colleagues that suit you.

- **You may answer, "Not now," to <u>Adapting Your Style?</u>** because your style of approaching the work is getting you the **success** and positive feedback you desire.

You don't have to be perpetually in the process of changing your work. There are pleasurable places along the career path that are worth enjoying fully. I was in one of those places in my career path when The Three Career Questions were born.

The humble birthplace of The Three Career Questions was in a rented conference room during a professional association meeting. The facilitator asked a room full of consultants to do the impossible: "Define your work in terms of end-results that your clients experience. Use no more than eight words."

Well, it felt not just impossible, but almost insulting to try to reduce something as complex as management and career coaching to eight words. But the facilitator was firm and insisted that it *could* be done. In fact, she insisted that it *had* been done by most successful consultants who produced services that clients deemed truly valuable and desired.

It worked. After about fifteen minutes of sweating, crossing out, rewording, and, most of all, picturing my clients' end-results from our work together, I produced—count 'em—eight words:

Help clients Move Up, Move Out, Adapt Styles.
     1   2   3   4   5   6   7   8

Write Now Exercise
Creating Your Eight Words

This is a mental and writing exercise worth trying in the generous margins provided in this book. Whether you're working independently or as an employee, you have to define your value concisely and simply enough for others to *get* you. Write your eight words. Define your work in terms of end-results that your internal or external customers experience. Use no more than eight words. Okay...ten. This exercise is worth more than you now realize. You be the judge when you have finished it. Don't hesitate to ask others for their perceptions.

Six Benefits for the Reader

Answering The Three Career Questions: Your Lifetime Career Management System looks at the cycle of questions that must be answered multiple times throughout a lifetime in order to become Career Self-Reliant and artfully construct a personally satisfying, working reality. Expect to experience insights and impacts while reading this book and experimenting with your resulting thoughts and feelings. This book will:

1. **Reveal** the cycle of career management that spans a lifetime. This new, big picture view will enable you to **address the right questions at the right times**—constituting the first variable in the formula for success. It's what the skilled therapist, physician, business consultant, or career consultant does: ask the compelling and insightful questions at a time that the questions can help to guide action.

2. **Provoke** you with a tool box of questions to:
   - explore your own thinking and desires about work;
   - form new beliefs that enable actions beneficial to your career.

The book will provide compelling, personal questions contributed from clients and students I have encountered in my years of consulting work.

3. **Inspire** you to create conversations and inquiries about satisfying work within your network of colleagues and with trusted coaches, consultants, and teachers. Getting out of your own head and into dialogue with others will produce better insight and more action.

4. **Explore** underlying wisdom and trends that make these questions crucial for you now.

5. **Validate** you, the reader. Your questions are similar to the ones others ponder. Your questions will gain validity and utility as you read how others have heard inner questions that moved them to take action. During our work lives, we answer these questions more than once—not because our initial answer was wrong, but because these questions act as guiding career constants in the swirling Tornado of life-time work circumstances.

6. **Dare** you to write down some of the thoughts, suggestions-to-self, and insights right on these pages. Think of these notes as your repository of words or phrases that will enable you to act on relevant parts of the book—without having to reread or rescan the book later. You'll literally be able to flip the pages and find your own writing on the usable insights and actions you gleaned from this book. This feeds *your* strategy. Keep a pen and sticky-notes with this book.

APOLOGIES TO THE DIGITAL READER. In addition to your reader device you'll need an instrument called a *pen* and a piece of what is called *paper* to accept the dare of documenting your responses to the questions and exercises posed throughout the book. But PLEASE find a way to document your responses to these dares.

Before You Get Started: Assessing Which Question Is Most Compelling for You at This Time

This tool will help you establish a baseline for where you are today, and will provide clues about which of The Three Career Questions you are most drawn to at this time. Check a total of any twelve (12) questions below that are similar to the questions you've been asking yourself about your job or work situation. See which column has the highest number of checkmarks. Then, see the bottom of the table to determine which of The Three Career Questions seems to capture the personal career challenge that's most heavily on your mind. Don't look at the bottom first.

?	Check box	?	Check box	?	Check box
Why can't this person understand my point of view?		Why did my boss move to another city?		Will I be able to utilize my skill set here?	
Have I tried all ways of communicating I can think of? Are there more?		Why did the senior member of our group switch to another team?		Why isn't this fun anymore?	
Have I asked others for perspective/ideas?		Why was the structure of this team changed with practically no discussion or input from us?		Why did this challenge me in the past but not now?	
How can I succeed wearing all these hats?		Why is our product sales and marketing team not going after new customers?		What's next?	

What is "success" to me?		Where can I go if the next logical step is a position that is filled for the foreseeable future?		Where is the "horizon"—the challenge?	
Will collective teamwork ever work with my style?		If we operate better when supervision is gone, why would I want to "advance" to that role?		Am I losing ground in this role?	
How can I Move Up if I don't know more about _____?		Will this organization continue to survive?		I want to be a great manager. Is now the right time?	
Why don't the new people ask me for help or advice?		How do I get more control of this situation?		Am I capable of management responsibility here, or should I move to another organization?	
How can I seem older to gain the credibility with the older peer-group?		Am I doing work that virtually anyone could do?		What is there to learn now?	
Am I being too critical of others because I'm feeling critical of myself?		Why does this not feel like my tribe?		Have I learned everything I can from this position?	
How can I use what I know about other people's personalities (from these personality assessments we did together) to change the way I communicate with them?		Would I even want a promotion if I got one?		Why are we discussing this again? I thought we resolved this issue.	
TOTAL # CHECKED		TOTAL # CHECKED		TOTAL # CHECKED	

Adapt	Move Out	Move Up

Note: Tools or questionnaires such as this are available at the website for your future use.
www.3questionsconsulting.com

Why This Work Matters to Me

The nobility of work in all its forms is my fascination. Always has been. I've watched it become a passion, a pain, an inspiration, a consolation and an obsession for many. The special magic of skill + style (what I call "Skyle," which we'll discuss later) come together to make each person a "talent," not just a worker or a professional. My talent and commitment, as well as this book, is dedicated to help you:

- Accurately identify what is unique about your talent;
- Get rid of outdated or inaccurate concepts about your Self or your work;
- Be more conscious of your Skyle;
- Align with work that honors who you are becoming.

In short, get at least half of what Sigmund Freud described as the characteristics of maturity: *loving and working.*

OVERVIEW OF OLD-WAY VS. NEW-WAY

You successfully transitioned from adolescence to adulthood by making—and then changing—most of the decisions and relationships you had made along the way. This ability to adapt turns out to be an awkward but essential skill that you likely have used unconsciously throughout your career. Now, I hope to help you use it more consciously.

In this book, I will introduce a new way to think about your career and manage it over your lifetime—to offer you a process that is more strategic than just *serial job-finding*.

Job searching, over and over again, after a layoff, personal resignation, or in a state of frustration, is not career management. *It's reactivity*. And this reactive process is sub-optimizing your time, talent, and energy.

This book will *not* manage your career. *You* will.

This book *will* give you a way to assess where you are in your career at any point. You will then get to decide which strategic—and sometimes challenging—actions to take. Or, you may decide to become more passive—waiting-and-seeing what the Universe dishes out. In either case, you'll proceed with more insight and a clearer model for managing your career. It all starts with the artful use of just Three Career Questions.

The best questions inspire the best answers. *Answering The Three Career Questions: Your Lifetime Career Management System* gives you the questions. It is then your responsibility to answer them with the help of your Self (focusing on your higher purpose—using your intuition and wisdom, and not just your intellect), and the people and information surrounding you in the marketplace of ideas. We'll examine methods and tools to help you extend your conversations and investigations into your marketplace. You'll be able to shop for new ideas and perspectives on work. In addition, we'll look at issues of timing and stages of career development, and how your understanding of those helps you choose the right questions to ask. But, if you're looking for more specific or easy answers instead of questions, you should probably stop reading this book now, close it, and consider re-gifting, recycling, or reconsidering the type of assistance you need and why you thought it was going to help you.

Perhaps you thought the book might offer very specific advice or formulas. For example: "If you've just experienced (blah, blah, blah) for seven consecutive months in your job, then you should consider a promotion. But if (yahda yahda) has happened, then you should consider a lateral move within your organization instead." It is tempting to seek or disseminate this sort of prescriptive direction to solve all job woes or answer all career questions. The more experienced professional, however, rejects such simplistic, formulistic advice. Our business bookshelves are loaded with *answers* that worked for someone else at some other time and under some circumstances other than the ones you're probably facing right now. **This book instead provokes an ongoing relationship with *questions*. We will be harnessing your ability to better use those questions—while also tapping into your colleagues and the market context to manage your career. The best part is, you can use this method from where ever you currently are in your development.**

There will be key terms and concepts throughout the book. I'll repeat their use and remind you of their definitions throughout the chapters since many readers will pick up the book periodically (as needed in their career management) or dive into the chapter that looks most relevant to them rather than read the whole thing at once—thereby learning and retaining all the terms as they read.

> You'll also see an unusually wide page margin. This intentional design feature is to enable you to take notes and complete certain brief exercises without needing a workbook or extra paper.

The intent here is to learn the art of asking a few good questions at the right times. Good therapists, lawyers, consultants, and healthcare professionals do this each day of their professional lives. We go to these people—not just because of their knowledge or abilities—but because their diagnostic questioning enables them to surface the right knowledge and apply the right solution at the appropriate time. The good ones are efficient as well as effective.

We've all probably known one such professional who should have turned the questions around for self reflection. You, yourself, may be an astute professional who is insightful and curious with others, but ironically blocks the notion of probing your own thoughts and feelings—or perhaps forgets to do so. You may not be asking tough questions about your work and career—or your diet, finances, will and testament, business processes, drinking habits, haircut, or choice of associates. Think of reading this book as your chance to discover some compelling questions about your work that are so meaningful that you will want to discuss them with trusted others to gain clearer perspective and feedback.

Answering The Three Career Questions: Your Lifetime Career Management System is the operator's manual for individuals who are becoming Career Self-Reliant and striving to position themselves for work in a great organization with talented leadership. This book is the individual's guide to becoming conscious and clear about her own talent in order to better thrive under a great manager—or better defend her career against poor management. In this book, you will learn a model for owning and managing your career—not just today—but over a lifetime.

Tornado at the Crossroads

You keep having these persistent conversations with yourself. Over and over again, you question how work is going and keep examining information or situations around you to see if there is any "answer" for what to do next. Then, the phone rings, or your daughter comes to ask you for something, or a colleague enters your office or..., or...—any of a million distractions happen, and you stop the career conversation in your head.

But about twenty minutes or two hours later, you start to spin up the same conversation in your head. The same career information and situations come to mind—day after day—and they enter your mental Tornado. Day after day, you feed the Tornado.

Certain tough or complex career management decisions often circulate in our thinking, over and over—in that Tornado. Much like in a real tornado, our mental Tornado contains valuable material. But when we suck up informational debris off the landscape and just keep spinning it with no productive end result, we develop a sense of burnout, fatigue, and discouragement. And daily distractions and responsibilities guarantee that, every time we get into the Tornado, we'll get pulled away from our thoughts, and the Tornado will subside—for a while. Sound familiar? And tedious?

This book and the conversations it prepares you to have with trusted others will help you wrangle your mental Tornadoes to the ground, sort out the contents to find the value, and build as well as sustain a better career with the contents you preserve. *You need to stop the spin. It represents only mental busyness, but not career management.*

Consider these questions:

1. ***The Tornado.*** Did you see movie *Twister*? Are you just picking up more informational "debris" off the career landscape, or are you getting practical, personal, as well as critical market information to design your personal strategy?

2. ***Spinning the information?*** Do you find yourself coming back to the same "career conversation in your head" but never finishing it? *Get the conversation going outside of your own head.*

3. ***Are you problem-solving when you should be decision-making?***

Good analyzers and problem solvers (engineers, financial professionals, R&D-types) love this one. They just keep gathering data to "solve the problem" even when data is not the issue—decision making is. Sometimes knowing your deeper needs, personal strivings, values, and even professional fears can pull together the valuable elements that have been swirling amidst the debris in the Tornado—and enable you to decide on a fulfilling course of action.

If you really want to see problem solvers or analyzers struggle and waste time, give them options, choices, or decisions that are not broken and not a problem—they're just options. Their challenge is to know and choose what they want. Nothing has to be solved or fixed. It can be painful to watch these folks try to turn choice making into problems that they can solve.

You're at a career crossroads. There are three directions you can travel from here:

1. **You can Move *Up*** if you like the work and/or the organization that you work for and are finding success there.
2. **You can Move *Out*** if there is no longer a fit with the work, the boss, or the organization.
3. **You can *stay and Adapt Your Style*** if you like the work but aren't getting the success you desire and are capable of.

These choices represent The Three Career Questions, which we will discuss throughout this book.

"Landing a Job" Got You Into This Situation

If the Tornado at the Crossroads felt hauntingly familiar, rest assured; you're in good and plentiful company. The Tornado at the Crossroads phenomenon frequently distracts professionals starting in their late twenties all the way to their late fifties.

By the time most professionals are in their late twenties, they have had enough work experience to start raising deeper career questions like:

- "Is this all there is for the next forty years?"

- "Have I made a terrible mistake by choosing this profession/industry/business function as my source of work?"
- *"Patent law*? What was I thinking?" (Substitute "patent law" with occupations such as engineering, accounting, human resources, insurance sales, graphic arts, forestry management, manufacturing operations, or any of hundreds of occupations that people can come to doubt in terms of their fit over the long-term.

How do we get into this time and energy wasting mental Tornado of doubt, distraction, and indecision with our careers? Two metaphorical words capture the cause: "planets" and "parachutes."

The old version of career management involved just "launching your career," followed by job search techniques or serial job finding over a lifetime that would land you on the next Planet Job.

Blast-off: Headed for the Next Planet Job! (Career Tip: Never put an open flame this close to your butt and call it a "strategy.")

Let's look at some of the downsides embedded in this launching approach to job searching:

- It involves a heroic, one-shot effort (prone to foster over-commitment to one type of work or search strategy).
- It doesn't offer a lot of control over direction and navigation (is not designed to accommodate changes in direction or length of job search).
- It doesn't come with brakes (there is no safe way to stop anywhere along the process and hover).

"Landing a job" brings up the next antiquated symbol of job search and career management that can get us into the mental Tornado: **the parachute**.

"I've Landed! Now What?"

When we land on Planet Job, we land hard, take off the parachute, and abandon the rocket propulsion (our network). We often execute a plan to colonize, not just visit, Planet Job. This works until there isn't enough occupational oxygen to support life, or the atmosphere on Planet Job starts to become toxic. This model is built on the notion that we land a job and stay there. When the job stops being a fit, we have to substantially rebuild our means of leaving (rocket building materials = network, contacts, market research, resume, bio, etc.). We have to re-invest our time in market research and reaching out to our network to help pull us off Planet Job, out of its gravitational pull, and onto the **next** Planet Job.

The need for a Three Career Questions strategy often becomes clear at this time. Without first examining the questions about Moving Up or Adapting Your Style, you may go to considerable effort to get off of Planet Job, when doing so wasn't really necessary to get what you needed.

This traditional over-focus on Moving Out and job hunting, without career management strategy to accompany it, results in the Tornado at the Crossroads phenomenon that squanders your time and energy as it distracts you with doubts and half-considered ideas. When you consider people who jump from job to job over their whole working lives, you glimpse the short-sighted phenomenon representing the opposite of career management: serial job-finding.

Career Management is Not Serial Job-Finding

Key Terms

A Career is a sequence of experiences in the world of work with objectives and consequences." SEARS, S. (1982), "A Definition of Career Guidance Terms: A National Vocational Guidance Association Perspective." *Vocational Guidance Quarterly*, 31: 137–143.

Career Management is the art of managing one's relationship to work, over a lifetime, by maximizing insights that are intrapersonal, interpersonal, and market-based—and turning them into action strategies and experiences.

Career management is best approached like a good friendship or marriage. We adapt friendships and marriage relationships to sustain them over a long duration. The same is true of a healthy career strategy. We adapt it to keep it going over time. Regardless of our job at any particular moment, a career management strategy considers the wider space around us and the future-scape in front of us. It creates the personal, occupational Big Picture.

Key Term

Serial Job-Finding is what most people wind up doing instead of career management. Think of this approach as *repeatedly finding one-job-in-a-row*. It's like a parachute. You only use it one-time-in-a-row.

Lacking a more comprehensive strategy, people tend to strive for longevity in a job or organization to avoid facing their lack of a bigger career picture. This often devolves into defending their occupational borders against the natural forces of change. It also often involves striving to protect or sustain an earlier, a perhaps outdated, story about who they are as professionals. This is a dangerous version of career mismanagement. If all these individuals know how to do is strive harder at jobs that may not even fit who they are becoming, they are likely to be left behind.

Serial job-finding then becomes the reaction to market and organizational forces. It becomes the default strategy—and a replacement for true career management. While some may create a series of jobs that become fulfilling and lucrative, many more have found one job after another resulting in little more than a survival strategy.

The Three Career Questions strategy enables us to think a few moves ahead while anticipating and preparing for changes, thereby gaining some marketplace advantage (over the one-job-in-a-row, survival strategists).

As you read more about The Three Career Questions, think of them as a combination of a mantra and a career navigational guidance system. As The Three Career Questions cycle in your awareness and thinking, they will cause you to be more conscious of where you are in your "career space." Once this awareness is built, you will have a clearer idea of what constitutes your personal definition of success, and you can make course adjustments. **This book will help you define where you are while helping you plan your next moves.**

PART I:

PREPARING YOURSELF FOR
THE THREE CAREER QUESTIONS

CHAPTER 1:

WHY *QUESTIONS* INSTEAD OF *ANSWERS*?

This is not just a book about The Three Career Questions. It's also about the general value of questions in our thinking. How do our questions (or lack of them) limit or expand learning about who we're becoming or how we work? Fields ranging from software engineering to law utilize the art of questioning—a science in and of itself which has been studied and honed by philosophers throughout time. So, as you can surmise, questions and the art of questioning are pretty crucial to the process of discovering information about our surrounding world.

Some Assumed Truths About Questions to Get Us Started

Before we delve into The Three Career Questions, let's establish some basic truths about questions that will lay the groundwork for the rest of this book:

- Questioning can be an indirect way of expressing desire. Asking a lot of questions about a new car usually tips the salesperson that you reeeeeeeeeeally want it.
- Questioning can be a way of acknowledging that you lack or need something.
- Asking too many questions may denote weakness out on the street or in the office, while instead signifying strength in the laboratory, design studio, or in business consulting.
- Each profession designs and uses questions uniquely. Compare the questions of a courtroom attorney to those of a therapist, and you likely will note contrasting delivery style, content, and goals.
- A lack of questioning is dangerous and can lead you into work or relationships that don't fit who you're becoming.

- Weak or inadequate questioning of others regarding their perception of your work performance denies you the feedback-rich environment required for success today.
- Questions can be used to construct and/or deconstruct knowledge; a questioner may act as a seeker and/or as a teacher/mentor.
- Questions usually come about when:
  - Someone is curious about you or your knowledge/story;
  - Someone is challenging you or your knowledge/story.

What we learn and know depends on what we ask and how we ask it. With our search for meaningful work throughout our lives, we're taught and trained to ask about jobs. *Where are they? How do I apply to get one? What are the capabilities I need to qualify?* This relatively tactical approach to matching knowledge, skills, and abilities (KSAs) to an existing job description is common, historical, yet sometimes quite limited in its ability to produce satisfaction.

I want to expand the boundaries of what you can know about yourself and the work around you. I will empower you to ask the right questions at the right times so you can better act on your own behalf when it's time to Move Up, Move Out, or Adapt Your Style.

One way to better equip yourself to navigate these transitions is to ask more and better questions rather than running away in a hyperactive fit of "trying a bunch of stuff." Experimenting is not bad, but it does consume time and resources; I want to help you reduce the number of "experiments" or "false starts" with work that really doesn't serve YOU.

The Three Career Questions offer a toolkit for engaging in an ongoing *cycle* of mindful career assessment. We're all assessing our careers, but few are doing so very consciously. The Three Career Questions operate as a system to keep us constantly aware of our immediate options. This consciousness enables us to anticipate changes in our work-life and harness the changes rather than simply react to them.

The Three Career Questions do not, however, represent a formula for delivering rigid answers or solutions. Solutions are as personal and numerous as readers and their work situations. Instead, we will seek the best questions to trigger our best critical thinking. Simply put, higher quality questions foster the best thinking, and the best thinking produces the best decisions. The Three Career Questions represent a method of approaching the very broad topic of, "How am I doing and what might I do next?" and using the answers to achieve greater clarity and results.

I assume that you already can create solutions on your own or seek trusted advisors to assist you in developing a personally-relevant action plan or solution. Later in the book, we'll discuss who some of these chosen resources might be if you do not already have them or know who they are. The Three Career Questions then become a framework to provoke the kind of awareness, conversations, and analysis that bring you unique answers based on your personal context or frame of reference. You can then create an action plan or ask directly for necessary advice and counsel.

But stay mindful of this caution: good questions may lead to answers or strategies, but these answers and strategies subsequently change. As good and as carefully considered as the answers are at any one time, answers or career strategies eventually wear out. They easily become obsolete, not because they were the wrong decisions or actions, but because we live in a terribly dynamic work culture. The shelf-life of a strategy for a job for individuals age twenty-five to thirty-four is in fact about five years (Bureau of Labor Statistics, "Economic News Release," Sept. 18, 2012.).

The Problem with Questions: Letting Yourself Off the Hook

I'd like to inoculate you against the problem I found with using questions as a guidance system. Hopefully you'll be able to catch yourself if you, too, try this. When asking myself questions—hard questions—I often tended not to pursue the answers if left alone with no one to push me. This would be a good place to insert a whining voice complaining, "But it's haaaaaaaard." Or insert a more ironic, experienced, and jaded voice saying, "I'm too busy working at the job I hate to make time to find or develop the work I would like." These are both true statements, to varying degrees, for whoever is doing the whining. *And they're both traps.*

Questions can be annoying, whether they come from others or ourselves. Let's face it; they're a call to exert mental effort, and they might reveal ignorance, risk aversion, inexperience, or worse. They can lead to brilliant "ah ha" moments of insight just as easily as they can puzzle and entangle us. This book will help you befriend questions more and defend against them less.

Bad News (the Tornado) and Good News (Intuition)

One other thought habit gets in the way of answering The Three Career Questions, and that is *information overload.* Have you ever seen images of massive tornadoes photographed by storm chasers? These monster tornadoes pick up the contents of whole lives, farms, neighborhoods, and businesses, and carry them off—spinning and spinning—and deposit them miles later. Similarly, the information Tornado that storms in your head collects more and more data debris from the informational landscape—but just keeps spinning it.

Now think about some of the career conversations in your own head. Lots of ideas, questions, hearsay, facts, fears—all different voices are spinning in your continual, round-and-round discussion. Then, the phone rings, or someone walks into your office, or the bus stops, or your child asks you something—something interrupts the Tornado, and you shift to some other mental activity.

But then, minutes or hours or a day later—the same conversation starts to kick up in your head. The same mental debris starts spinning around; you're looking at it again, from every angle—not knowing how to make sense of it or push it away.

Now, let's turn to your intuition. It's like the storm chaser who knows there's valuable information, even knowledge, locked up in that twister. The fact that your Tornado won't go away is indicative of compelling questions about your work and career that you really want to answer even if you can't quite see or grasp them yet.

Both forms of information (intuition and data) are crucial to managing your career. So here are some recommendations about your Tornado.

Tornado Taming Tips	
The Problem	**What You Might Do About It**
1. The Tornado. You've seen the wild news videos of twisters vacuuming up towns and farms as they race across the landscape. Translate this image to your career: are you just picking up more random informational debris off the career landscape and spinning it? Or are you getting practical, personal, and critical market information to build a career strategy?	The Internet can be your best friend and worst enemy at this time. The Tornado is indiscriminate in terms of what it collects. Books and consultants offer models of how information or ideas fit together and key words that help you describe the world around you. You will need to start getting selective about the information you notice. Later in the book, we'll talk about two tools to aid in this process: 1) A Focus Of Inquiry and 2) A KISSA analysis of yourself.
2. ***Spinning the information***? Do you find yourself coming back to the same career conversation in your head but never finishing it?	It's time to engage someone outside of the Tornado spinning in your head. Create dialogue with others and explore the contents of your thinking. Outsiders can slow and eventually stop the Tornado with the right questions to aid decisions or values clarification.
3. Are you problem-solving when you should be ***decision-making***? Good problem solvers (engineers, financial professionals, industrial designers) love this one. They just keep gathering data to "solve the problem" even when data won't fix it. They're just adding to the Tornado.	Sometimes knowing your needs, personal strivings, values, and even professional fears, can break the logjam, enable decision making, and calm the Tornado. Personal and professional values are what you use to make choices and decisions. Are yours unconscious? It may be time to clarify them—out loud.

When data and your intuition start to either spin or overload, it's time to invite trusted others into your career conversation.

Here's a quick example. Let's say you have a department administrator who is quite the free spirit. The department is slow moving and not advancing. So he gives notice and starts planning an odyssey to study French and learn a unique form of boat building on the Normandy coast. You're more than a bit envious. A year or two later, you run into him in the grocery store. In a friendly voice, he asks, "What are you still doing in that (job and organization)?" He means it as a sort of compliment, but it eats at you. You know this colleague's question is compelling for some reason, because it won't leave your mind. You just don't completely know why. This is when you have to listen to the (sometimes annoying) wisdom of your intuition—that inner force which knows when it's time for questioning and change. When the path is not clear to you, this is when it can be helpful to search out-loud with a trusted friend, colleague, or coach.

Managing your career cycle is a constant process of inquiry and experiment. There are two forms of information and knowing available to help you form a career strategy: data and intuition. But these two forms don't always play well together in your head.

We start with the assumption that your intuition about your Self and your work is valuable—if sometimes under-utilized or even ignored. Some consider this sixth sense or "knowing without knowing" to be another form of intelligence. Daniel Goleman, in his October 2, 2007, blog entry, "Moral Intuition," posed a great question that exemplifies intuition kicking in to help with our perception of situations or dilemmas. He also explains what intuition feels like. (See DanielGoleman.info).

As Goleman says in his October 2007 blog, "Consider the essential moral question, 'Is what I am about to do in keeping with my values, ethics, or *sense of meaning*?'" (For our purposes in this book, think *"meaning of work."*)

He also states, "I've argued that the answer to this query comes to us first as a felt sense of 'rightness' or 'wrongness,' and only afterward do we explain to ourselves why this might be so. In Social Intelligence (the same blog), I described the mid-brain circuits of the 'low road,' which manages such spontaneous, automatic responses to life. These neural systems are thickly connected to the brain's emotional centers and the gut—but not to the thinking brain, the neocortex. Our first moral response comes as a feeling, not a thought. And in *Emotional Intelligence* (Bantam 2006), I argued that our capacity for self-awareness and reflection lets us better attune to such signals, which can be subtle."

You will encounter questions from your reading and discussions with others that create opportunities for you to listen to your intuitive reactions. Listen quietly and carefully to your body as well as your mind in this process. Slight (or strong) feelings of discomfort are clues to something that needs further inquiry. Use the discomfort as a catalyst to continue exploring. If the discomfort discourages you, use it as motivation to design a new coping and adaptation strategy.

Where to Take the Questions and Answers You Don't Like: Sources of Help

Some questions seem to resist reasonable answers. ("What is the perfect job for me?") Similarly, some answers seem too difficult or awkward to implement. (You learn that you need a PhD to get your ideal job. Do you want to start that at age fifty-nine?) If you find yourself struggling with either or both of these, you're probably wasting lots of time in Tornado conversations with yourself (spinning up the same conversations and reviewing the same information without coming to a resolution or action).

At times like this, we all need what I call a Think Out Loud Laboratory (TOLL). This is the place you take the questions that seem to resist clear answers. This is also the place you take the answers that you don't like, don't trust, or don't understand. This is a real place with real people, and it's outside your head. This is a place where you can hear your own voice saying surprising things— sounding curious and even naïve. This is a place with at least one trusted mammal present. It may be your Golden Retriever sitting in for your manager, partner, or significant other if things are not going well. But ideally, a trusted other listens and asks you questions rather than compulsively offering advice.

Why the TOLL? What's the big deal? Well, it turns out that talking and thinking use two different brain processes. But this is significant for you in discovering what you really want and believe about your work. We've all experienced the difference between the clarity of a thought and the clarity of speech about that thought: the job interview. *We've all been there.*

Picture this. The interviewer asks a question about a relevant problem that must be solved in the company, and your brain says, "Yes, I've got this one nailed. I've solved this one fifty times." And then your mouth flies open, and you hear yourself saying something quite different than your previous, confident thoughts about the problem—and it's sounding pretty disorganized. And it gets worse. You also don't know where you're going to end your answer. You've never actually *heard* yourself organize and say this information for anyone outside of your head.

Okay, wake up. The nightmare is over. You're not really in the interview watching the interviewer's eyes roll back in her head as she dozes off in the middle of your ramble.

But here are some similarities between the poorly prepared talent trying to manage his career questions in his head and the interviewee who has never answered tough questions out loud (nor audibly told his accomplishment stories to anyone before the interview): they are both over-relying on cognitive process. They are both missing the preparation for speech, the mental rigor of dialogue—carefully converting thoughts into language that can be understood by others. When we convert thoughts to spoken language, we discover additional nuances of our meaning, values, and credibility.

So Who Are the People in Your Think Out Loud Laboratory?

Here are some suggestions.

- **Friends or Colleagues Who Have Moved Out, Moved Up, or Adapted Their Style**. These are the people who should populate your network and provide much of the insight and perspective you'll need. Remember, they're sharing their perspective and experience—not a clairvoyant, all-knowing perspective on marketplace reality or what your next move should be. They, through a collective series of conversations and dialogues, also represent the ambient IQ and emotional intelligence of the marketplace at this time. You need to tap that ambient "knowing" distributed out there, rather than come to over-rely on your own perceptions or a limited few online sources. This is why career consultants will push and nudge you into the marketplace of ideas where you can dialogue with your friends and colleagues—including those to whom they will introduce you.

Write Now Exercise
Kick-Starting Your TOLL

After reading this section, I will ask you to start creating your TOLL. For now, jot down the names of a few individuals who are currently in your mind. Go ahead, dog-ear the page, and then jot some names here. In fact, write all over the inside of this book. *Career management is not just a concept; it's the various acts required to get both what you need and what you want throughout a lifetime of work. Recording your perceptions and intentions for future reference is essential to this process. Your experience gaining insights from this book will compete with all the other demands of mundane, other-directed work life. Why not give your perceptions an advantage by writing them down here or somewhere so you can come back to them?*

- **Mentor or Manager at Work**. Be careful here. Let's not be too naïve about the process of conducting a genuine inquiry into your career options within your current workplace. Your mentors and managers work for an organization. They owe it some loyalty as well as rely upon it to support them. They may be less than thorough in their ability or willingness to help you Move Out of the organization if their productivity (read "bonus") is tied to having key talent (you) stay for another year or two—or four. If you're in a very constricted industry or organization, it may be an awkward conversation for the manager who feels impotent or empty-handed while engaging in a hopeful "Move Up" discussion with you.

  The "Moving Up" discussion is a bit less risky, however, if the manager has opportunities to discuss with you. In more progressive organizations that really understand talent management, you'll in fact have no trouble triggering this conversation. In fact, your manager or mentor will probably trigger it without you having to ask. This type of organization is rare and worth considering as a worthy, longer-term site for your professional development.

- **Professional, Trained Career Management Consultants**. These are your most versatile career strategy partners, assuming they have some marketplace experience. I think a consultant who is only academically experienced in the process of career consulting can be somewhat helpful, but not as much as one with work experience in a functional business area (perhaps finance, human resources, sales, operations) and even management experience (perhaps within government, a non-profit, an international organization—or whatever your target work culture is becoming).

- **Counselor or Therapist.** These professionals are unlikely to become a solid source of thorough or long-term career strategy. Why? Lack of business training and experience is the most frequent reason. The rigor required to be a therapist usually requires intensive academic study, internships, sometimes licensing, supervised clinical experience, and then the joys of learning the world of insurance reimbursement or government funding for community-based counseling programs. All of this study and activity allocates very little time and focus for studying and strategizing about business models or a range of careers and workplace cultures.

Therapists are best used for managing your uncomfortable reactions or need for coping skills in stressful work situations. Most therapists recognize their lack of preparation in the area of career strategy and lack of experience in work settings, and they'll refer clients to career consultants after they've helped reduce and manage anxiety, depression, or angry reactions to a colleague or work situation. You can benefit greatly from getting your therapist and career consultant to exchange perspectives and history about their work with you. Too often, we see counselors, healers, and consultants happy to work in their own silos of perceptions about their clients—while assuming they each see the whole picture. You, the client, lose time and efficiency in your use of professional help when valid information about your style is not shared among everyone trying to further your success. Sign a release of information form with every professional, and ask them to have a brief exchange of information about their perceptions and goals of counseling or consulting with you.

- **Professor/Teacher/Instructor.** Really rely on these folks to know where former students have gone to work and prospered—or suffered in the workplace. They can be a rich resource in your network-driven market research. But there may be a limit to some academics' perspectives. When you think about when they come into contact with talent, it's usually just before the talent graduates and goes on to a first or next job. But they often have little ongoing contact with people deep in their careers over time. Career centers at universities and colleges are great at preparing people to launch, but are still evolving deeper experience and knowledge about navigating the rapids of the workplace once a graduate is out in the work stream.

Most important of all, however, faculty and career center professionals connect you to alumni. Your alumni network is already out there, and as a graduate, you are officially a member of this inner circle. *Use it. Make contacts.* If nothing else, it's a benign place to start your networking-driven market research with people who are predisposed to give you a break since you're members of the same tribe.

- **Spouse/Partner/Person You're Dating.** There's a reason therapists and physicians don't treat their own families: dual relationships. *You really can't be objective, direct, and credible with someone who sees you in some of the garb you sleep in (or don't sleep in).* The people we live with may have helpful perspective and ideas; and God knows they have opinions about our weaknesses! In a way, however, they know us too well, and may be less able to think of realistic possibilities with us. We've often worn out their abilities to be objective. And they often tire of the ongoing mental Tornado that we struggle with and share with them. *Go easy here.* You're dealing with a source of potential unconditional regard that will support you when your emotional state really needs it. Don't ask these folks to be experts or resources too often. Go instead to an outside, trusted resource who knows your career territory and the possibilities. Turn to those who have been asking and answering The Three Career Questions to manage their own careers.

As a final thought, in a rigorous career exploration you're likely to encounter a number of challenging questions and answers you don't like. If you choose to take them to a trusted other person for discussion, your chances of a more sophisticated and well-rounded solution increase. Ultimately, the marketplace will decide to offer you meaningful work, or not. Your networking driven research will become your core marketplace sample that will guide your moves toward meaningful work and away from situations that don't fit you. Research is first about questions. "Ah ha" moments and useful discoveries come later.

Write Now Exercise
Building Your Personal TOLL

Speaking of "Ah ha," this would be a good time to wander over to the ample margins and list the most reliable, trusted people you can turn to for career and marketplace perspectives. If this seems difficult, or practically no one comes to mind, consider writing a couple of places you can visit to meet such people (for example, professional associations, alumni events, business speaker events, job search support groups, etc.)

CHAPTER 2:

METAPHORS FOR YOUR CAREER: STORIES, SHAPES, CYCLES AND ORBITAL MECHANICS (ORBITAL WHAT?)

Personal Career Theory

John Holland, a pioneer in the understanding of career management and career decision making, wrote about the idea of a Personal Career Theory (PCT). We all have one. Yours is now running in your head on both a conscious and subconscious level. Didn't know you were a theorist, did you? According to narrative psychology theory (Fisher 1987), we are all storytellers and listeners. Our world around us is made intelligible through stories that we are given by others and ones that we create and re-create as we live. Some are more reality based than others. Some work better than others as descriptions of what actually happens in our surrounding world. And some are mostly just about what happens inside our own heads.

Consider Nancy, a struggling environmental consultant with a solid analytical mind, Ivy League engineering degree, and lucrative job in a downtown engineering firm. Her early grades in math triggered a process whereby others began writing her career narrative. Her grades and test scores during high school were off the charts, and others began to presume when talking to Nancy that she would pursue a math-related career. Nancy joined this general consensus. Her Personal Career Theory (PCT) was founded on her notion, "If I test well in something, that's what I should be doing for a living. I'm engaged in work related to those high test scores, so I should be happy." Her math and science skills were perfect for pursuing a degree in civil engineering.

Well, her testing skills got her into college; her study skills got her through it; and four years later, she was working in a national environmental consulting firm. But she found herself eventually feeling like her job was "can do" work more than "want to do" work. At this point, we can say that Nancy's PCT, founded primarily on the basis of her grades and test scores, was falling short as a guiding theory of how to find satisfying work.

The revision or reconstruction of her PCT came with difficult realizations and hard work. She had to discover a whole body of feelings, interests, and values that had been glossed over at an earlier developmental stage when engineering had been the career presumed by others as well adopted as her Personal Career Theory.

Nancy began to review the high-satisfaction experiences of her life—both in and out of work, as well as before and after college. An important factor emerged: *people*. Interpersonal contact, teamwork, public speaking, and persuasion were involved in so many of the projects that she had enjoyed and done successfully.

Her new, more-consciously-revised PCT included additional, mature insights about what interested and motivated her. This process diversified her awareness of her strengths and emotions while enhancing her ability to make choices that would include new kinds of work activities and relationships. Her updated PCT was one that reflected Nancy's current work reality (wherein she experienced boredom with quantitative work contrasted to energy during interpersonal engagements with staff or clients). Her new PCT also expanded to realize a broader range of potential work roles—enabling her to exit the rut she had been in and progress to a fuller expression of who she could be personally and professionally.

A theory—or in this case, a Personal Career Theory—is a system of ideas intended to explain phenomenon we see in the world around us.

> ## Key Term
>
> A **Personal Career Theory** is a set of ideas used to antici-
> pate and estimate the results of a career choice, so that you
> don't have to approach every situation as novel—reasoning
> through it from scratch.

Use your own PCT with a note of skepticism, however, because
as a theory, it's being tested, and it may adapt over time (as
Nancy's did). In fact, part of good career management involves
setting up a solid, feedback-rich environment for yourself, and
then using that feedback to validate your theory—or invalidate it
and construct an updated one. I'll get into this idea of the feedback
rich environment in more depth in the chapter on "Adapting Your
Style for Greater Success."

Personal Stories or Narratives

Another way that we organize and store our thinking about something, instead of constructing a theory, is by creating a story, or
narrative, about it. Much like Fisher (1987), John Holland (1997)
refers to the (PCT) as a mental description or story that we all
develop to explain our perception of how career choices and
results play out over time. When the personal narrative or story
that accompanies our PCT doesn't seem to provide an adequate
context for the events or strivings that are emerging in our work
lives, we often seek help in the form of a coach, mentor, or advisor.

We tend to screen out stories, facts, and even observations that
are not congruent with the selective perception that accompanies
our current stories or theories. This is why we often need the reality checks and course corrections that can be stimulated by someone outside of ourselves giving us feedback.

Feedback, dialogue, and assessment tools (personality assessments, interest inventories, etc.) are designed to:

- Assist you with insight into your current work identity;
- Differentiate what Drake (2007) refers to as the *available stories* offered by our context, history, culture, family and even vocabulary and the *potential stories* that can be created or co-created for a more congruent or fulfilling future;
- Explain or normalize the shifts in identity that occur with development, trauma, new relationships, changes in the marketplace, and age;
- Expand your possibilities to create new identities through the creation or co-creation of new narratives about your work. These new narratives respect the shifts or changes that are taking place in and around you, creating a story that fits who you're becoming.

The re-crafting of one's story can be particularly challenging for the individual who is shifting his or her work identity to a new career, not just a new job. Ibarra (2004) describes the three stages of career development that require an individual to create new stories about themselves as:

1. Seeker (collecting information and insights about possibilities);
2. In-between (experimenting with the new while still doing the old);
3. "Ex" (fully embracing the new work identity and leaving the old one behind).

Many people approach a career or job change with the naïve hope that it will be as easy and fast as switching from one to the other during a blinding flash of insight. As Ibarra cautions, "Don't wait for a cataclysmic moment when the truth is revealed. Use everyday occurrences to find meaning in the changes you are going through. Practice telling and retelling your story. Over time, it will clarify."

This re-crafting of one's story is where the career coach can add value, speed, and clarity. As a way to expedite information-gathering to understand a client's current story, career coaches frequently administer and interpret various assessments to measure personality preferences, values, skills, and interests. Coaches can use this data as an opportunity for their clients to look at other occupations utilizing the same interests—and see these other occupations not necessarily as what the person "should become," but rather as potential *clients, customers, or colleagues* in their future work. This process is like looking for one's lost tribe— the people who share a similar set of values, expectations, and ways of seeing the world of work.

Case Study
History Teacher Envisions New Work Team Members

Consider Pat, who is a history teacher and twenty-year veteran of the classroom, and whose Strong Interest Inventory (used to assess interest patterns) indicates similar interest patterns with occupations such as marketing executive, graphic artist, teacher, and technical writer. Pat reacts negatively to the notion of becoming a marketing executive, but the coach invites him to transform that reaction by thinking of the marketing executive not as a career goal, but as a possible teammate. "Suppose you're a member of an organization where you and a marketing executive occasionally work together in meetings or on projects," the coach says. Then, the coach has Pat re-narrate his story as: "Maybe I work for a textbook publisher, and I'm on a team with a marketing executive, a graphic artist, and a technical writer—working together to design a textbook cover that will get students interested in a book about history."

When coaches complete this exercise with their clients, they essentially have created the beginnings of alternative stories about the clients' working identities—starting with assessment-based data (as well as the coach's insights and observations), and projecting some of who the clients are or could be as inspired by some of that data.

Our PCT is the story or picture we have going on in "the movie theater of the mind," and it depicts what we think our career is supposed to be about. Because we tend to seek career assistance only after our current career *reality* is in conflict with the *story* or what's showing in our "movie theatre of the mind," it suggests a common foible we have come to know and love about ourselves and others: **we tend not to act strategically and in advance of career pain, but rather in response to it.**

As my clinical supervisor counseled me during my clinical internship, "People tend to change based on either psychological insight...or pain. Bet on pain. Most of your clients have been working on pain as their signal for knowing when it's time to change."

Using *Answering The Three Career Questions: Your Lifetime Career Management System* gives you the opportunity to be alert and sense issues that need to be questioned while they are in pre-pain stages (versus high-drama time). Think of these strategies as a method to head off a career migraine before it gets really painful.

Orbital Mechanics Versus "The Stairway to Heaven": New Physics of Career Management

As we tackle each of The Three Career Questions, we need to look at the new physics of managing a career over a lifetime of work. It no longer looks or feels the same as that which some of our elders and early role models demonstrated.

First, let's examine the potential shapes of your career—the visual metaphors for how things are evolving so far in your professional life. You may discover a form of geometry that describes the career model of your elders, but may be sensing that these shapes just aren't working for you. These shapes are analogous to your PCT—suggesting how you expect your career to function. You might sense that your PCT is not adequate to explain what seems to be happening, but an alternative model hasn't showed up yet. Maybe you'll have a model that makes contemporary sense by the end of this chapter.

We'll take a look at four shapes that are representative of some common careers. The fifth visual metaphor will represent a most contemporary version of how your career might work for optimum strategic benefit.

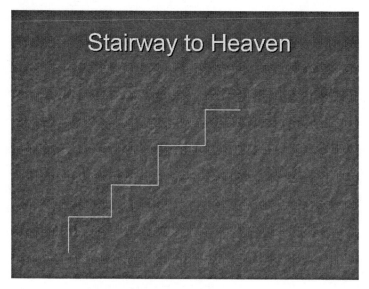

Stairway to Heaven

The traditional "go, and stay until you're asked to leave" model of career management is not without merit. It fits certain eras and types of organizations that dominated specific times. The rise of the corporation after WWII, and the command-and-control style of management that dominated our thinking at that time, made for very structured, orderly career paths. Organizations were competitively motivated, in the fifties, to attract and train talent. The War had caused a whole generation of manufacturing and design talent to delay mastery of much beyond war-related skills and management styles. So, the Stairway to Heaven was born— consisting of a clear path for advancement and complete training in management and other technical skills needed to build the post-War workforce. These steps were managed by the employer; programs were designed to recruit and move talent up through the corporate or government ranks to fill the seemingly endless need for more workers and managers.

The rules for individuals to participate in this form of career development were as follows:

- Think Big Co.—as in big organizations that had money for training and growth.
- "Color inside the lines," as described by your manager.
- Stay with the company for as long as you can.
- Leave only if you're told to (laid off).

As our business models changed in the 1990s, we saw downsizing, reorganization, process improvement, and the "projectizing" of work become the pervasive trends in many work cultures. These major changes signaled a slow death of many training and development programs that had previously fostered a generation or two of business and government leaders.

A crucial shaping force also came into play: how work got packaged. As work processes were better designed, company leaders realized that many jobs and processes didn't need to be permanent. Instead, they needed to be flexible, and they needed to be paid for only when needed. As a culture, we shifted—from assuming that work would include a set of ongoing behaviors performed by permanent functional groups or departments—to a definition of work that:

- Focused on results or outcomes;
- Then defined the work as a set of projects, each with a beginning and an end, that could be done by contractors, vendors, or robots—as well as regular employees.

Say goodbye to the Stairway to Heaven unless you're inside one of the few remaining organizations that bank on developing and retaining *key talent* (which is different from *all* talent). These include such hallmarks of manufacturing and leadership development as General Electric. Still, even if you find such a "Stairway" opportunity inside a private or public entity, be sensitive to your organization's revenue cycles of boom and bust and how those can wipe out access to training or technical certifications you may be counting on.

A tragic flaw developed inside of the Stairway model: *The Peter Principle.* Being promoted to one's level of incompetence became an unintended consequence of development programs that relied on time-in-position or seniority alone to move people into management or higher levels of complexity. Training programs eventually became optional or economically burdensome for many companies, and the Stairway to Heaven became more like a step closer to Hell for many who had to work with or for leaders who hadn't really developed their skills and competencies. With the eventual falling off of training or conscientious, action-based learning programs, aspiring managers were left to find and implement just-in-time solutions like, "...Just figger it out."

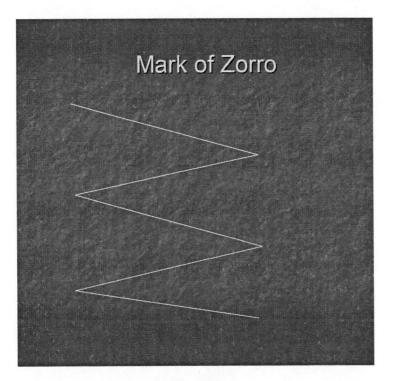

Mark of Zorro

If this shape resonates with your sense of your career path, you may have moved up in a large organization that had different subsidiaries or divisions where you could relocate and accumulate experience. Much as Zorro was riding off to different places to rescue good from evil, this model combines Moving Up (developing, not just getting promotions) and being geographically flexible. This model represents a great way to develop your talent using experience as the teacher and putting yourself in multiple new situations (subsidiaries, new acquisition, startups) to stretch and grow.

As broadening as this model can be, it comes with some career limits or cautions. For those who work in rapidly changing and competitive industries (such as high tech), staying too long in one company may brand you as hard to reorient to a new employer's culture. Others may worry that you will be prone to perceiving and doing things "...the way we used to at the Acme Ball Bearing Company," your former (and perhaps only) work culture. Managing or optimizing a career that's in this shape requires you to keep your knees bent and able to move flexibly; in other words, you must adapt quickly and innovate based on environmental changes.

Springboard to Success

The Springboard to Success model has worked well for those who enter legal or accounting professions and join a firm right out of school. They spend their careers as attorneys or CPAs and move up to partner roles, experiencing ever-higher levels of complexity and compensation within the same firms.

This model might also represent a career that starts and stays in one functional area of organizational work (finance, human resources, marketing, operations, surgery, counseling, etc.). For example, someone might start a career in human resources as a benefits representative and then move to employee relations, compensation, training, and other areas. Eventually, that person may lead one of those areas—and then a different area, and maybe a couple of areas simultaneously. Eventually, this person may become director or VP of the total human resources function.

What is the downside of this career management model? If you've achieved this by age forty-five, and this is the only function you've worked in, *it's likely to be the only function you're ever going to work in. You're positively, professionally branded.* It's been good to you, but it becomes limiting. If you move to a smaller market with few if any VP of human resources positions, your perceived ability to contribute to a smaller business, or on the operations side or other functional area of a larger business, could be in doubt. I've seen impressive talent move from Fortune 100 companies to a middle market city (population two million) with two Fortune companies and gasp for professional oxygen until they can breathe more slowly, learn to think small, and market themselves in downscaled ways.

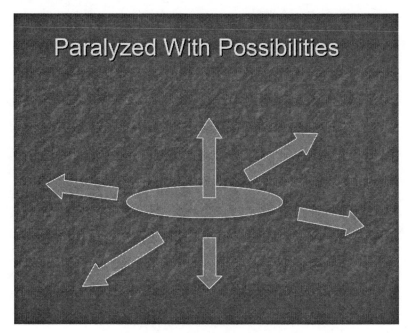

Paralyzed with Possibilities

Well-educated...experienced...good interpersonal and leadership instincts. All good, right? While it is great to have all these things going for you, you still may *feel* less than ideal. **Having multiple skills and strengths is often described by my clients as being in a "mental Tornado." The conversations in their head about what to choose and what to do next can become daunting.** As we described earlier in the book, these mental conversations start...then spin up lots of thoughts and facts and what-ifs. Then, inevitably, there is an interruption—a traffic signal changes, the phone rings, the baby starts to cry, or "You've got mail" beckons—and the conversations in their heads end. But then, three hours later, on the drive home, they spin up and start at the beginning again. Little or no progress is made while these clients just spin the same ideas and questions about potential options.

This shape often characterizes the feelings of a thirty-something professional who just has finished an MBA or a fifty-two-year-old with a successful career in finance. Both are ready to try something completely different, and *the possibilities are paralyzing them. They lack insights to guide them.* They can benefit from career conversations with a career coach or significant others to:

- Hear their own thinking;
- Test ideas in a Think Out Loud Lab (TOLL)—a safe, confidential place to broadcast all of their uncensored thoughts and feelings out loud.

The crucial success factor in navigating through this state is *time management*. You can only afford to stay paralyzed for so long. You can only afford to spin up those same conversations in your head so many times before needing to empty out the Tornado and take action. Professionals with very demanding leadership, technical, or service roles are famous for allowing their work or clients to demand all of their time and attention, leaving insufficient time to break out of the old thinking patterns, collect needed information, and implement personal action plans. They frequently find their ways to my office by way of astute therapists who have treated their depression, anxiety, or obsessive compulsive tendencies and said, "Your work on yourself is done for now. What you need is a change in your work. Call this person, and get a strategy."

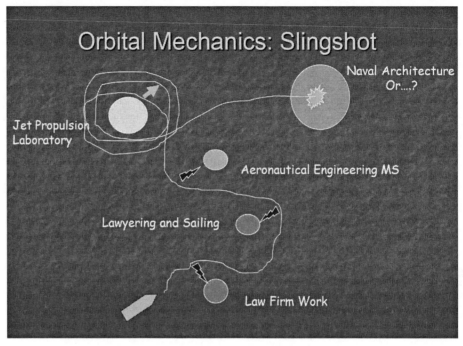

Orbital Mechanics: "The Gravitational Slingshot"

Think of yourself as an occupational space probe packed with instrumentation (your talents) to study and use in impacting various kinds of planetary conditions (employers, markets, job challenges). Your mission (your professional development over a lifetime) is to study certain planets, accumulate knowledge and the ability to make positive impact, and eventually meet the far reaches of the solar system (your maximum development as a professional). **Work is not usually a round trip; instead you go and go and go until you can't go any further or decide to stop. You seldom wind up back where you started.**

Problem: you only have so much endurance before your parts wear out—as a human or a space probe—and you can only carry so much fuel (the time you have to learn and earn your way to your highest level of work development). So, how can the new career physics help you go farther while saving fuel (time)? Orbital mechanics and the gravitational slingshot hold some valuable clues. These techniques help scientists determine how to get a spacecraft deep into our solar system without having to carry a lot of unnecessary fuel.

Let's look briefly at how it works in space. Then, we'll try applying it to your known universe—employment—and the time between your first and last job—as it creates the broader picture of your lifetime flight path of work.

Each planet has a gravitational field that attracts nearby matter. The closer you get to the planet, the stronger and faster you're pulled toward it. The trick in space travel is to use the pull of a planet, thereby preserving your precious, onboard fuel as the planet gives you additional speed in the direction you want to go. Then, all you have to do at a precisely timed moment is briefly blast your rocket engines just enough to adjust your direction, and off you'll go with a free boost of gravitational energy from your new favorite planet.

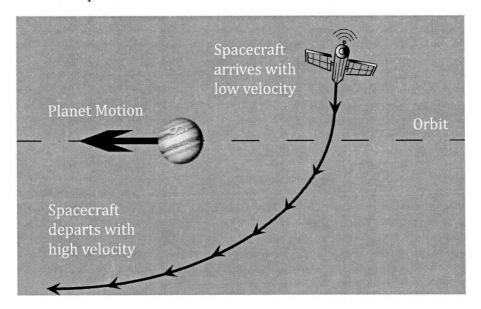

Disclaimer: At this point, I probably need to formally offer an apology to all the scientists who designed and executed the Cassini Project (and others like it, unknown to me), a true marvel of science and teamwork that used the principles of orbital mechanics to accomplish a fantastic photographic and research mission deep into our solar system. I have just borrowed, then over simplified, and perhaps corrupted, one of your prized principles of astrophysics! But thanks for the loan; I hope you can apply it to managing your own careers.

If we translate that concept of using orbital mechanics, or the "gravity slingshot", in our career strategy it means gaining energy, knowledge and enhanced professional capability from each organization you work for. It also means probably not becoming a permanent fixture there. Thinking ahead and having a career strategy means having some awareness of where you'd like this organization's energy and direction to propel you.

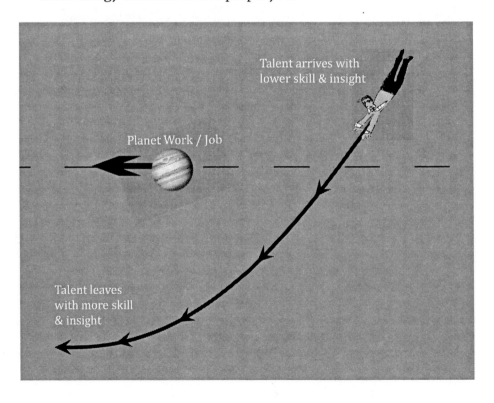

Talent arrives with lower skill & insight

Planet Work / Job

Talent leaves with more skill & insight

How Orbital Mechanics Came to Career Management

There is a coincidentally instructive case study attached to how orbital mechanics was revealed to me and then applied to career management. It's quite a coincidence that orbital mechanics became a metaphor for Harrison's career and one of the cornerstones behind how he eventually would design actual space missions. And talk about esoteric job titles! Try this one: "Senior Engineer Near-Earth Mission Architecture Group." Yes, that's a real job title.

This concept was explained to me in a deceptively casual conversation by Harrison, a person who had suffered a career struggle that, at times, felt a little like a slow motion train wreck over a decade or two. The concept of orbital mechanics seemed cool just by itself. But as he was describing the helpful forces of nature that could be harnessed to propel a space probe, it occurred to me that he was describing a strategy for managing our personal journey through a lifetime of work.

While ostensibly successful and financially secure, satisfaction with work had eluded Harrison for years. He suffered with a mismatch to an inherited family law practice, and followed it with a stint working as a mechanical engineer/intellectual property lawyer—a position exhausted by a wild ride of prosecuting dozens of patent infringements on one of the most famous inventions of our time: the laser. After this, he went to a large regional law firm and began wasting away in a culture that seemed to discourage all human contact among internal colleagues.

His sanctuary and inspiration was his beloved live-aboard sailboat. Its disproportionately high importance to him started to clue him in to what he missed at work and how draining the long work hours and days had become. He followed the cycle of "lawyering and sailing" with an acting stint—where he acted in a few plays, commercials, and was a movie walk-on while still practicing law. Law continued to disappoint, and Hollywood was, well, Hollywood; but the sailboat never disappointed.

Then came the reckoning: *it was time to stop experimenting and get deeper traction toward a work of passion.* He began to contemplate sail design and boat building. His networking-driven research pointed him to naval architecture as the logical next stage of career preparation. His perpetual appetite for learning and education started to re-ignite. But where were the naval architecture schools? Nowhere close to where Harrison and his wife and two children were living. But an encouraging and insightful piece of advice came from one of his networking partners: *the first couple of years of naval architecture studies closely resemble the content in an aeronautical engineering masters program.* Aeronautical engineering thus became his first action step.

Think of Harrison as an occupational space probe as he aspired to get to the heavenly body of Planet Naval Architecture. But now, the gravity of Planet Aeronautical Engineering pulled him and started to accelerate his progress, or slingshot him, in a slightly different but relevant direction. His investigation of Planet Aeronautical Engineering gave him information, skills, and a boost toward his ultimate destination of Naval Architecture.

As it turned out, when Harrison picked up that extra energy boost from the pull of Planet Aeronautical Engineering, he was able to pick up additional speed and momentum with a work opportunity he hadn't planned for: Planet Jet Propulsion Laboratory (JPL). And it was there that Harrison went into orbit for an extended amount of time. This transition marked a critical decision in terms of how he used his limited fuel ("time," in career management terms). Remember, he was headed to Planet Naval Architect. Recall what happens to objects that orbit around a planet for a long period of time: the gravity of the planet pulls them to the surface and crashes them—unless they have the fuel and motivation to blast out of orbit toward another destination. Would Harrison be at risk of staying too long and getting trapped by the gravitational pull and convenience of a great, well-resourced, institutional employer?

At this point, Harrison harnessed his sense of "mission architecture" as his decision-making guide. He envisioned a ten-year orbit around Planet JPL—wherein he could study and perfect his project management skills, learn design software, and even participate in ocean research (studies to better understand the capability of launching space vehicles from an ocean platform). During this process, he could also earn and save a fair amount of income and retirement funds—part of what it takes to survive after leaving the atmosphere of Planet Jet Propulsion Lab. Harrison's prior network-driven market research into his passion—nautical design work—had confirmed that, once out of his JPL orbit, he would possess the necessary skills to work at a sail loft and boatyard without first visiting Planet Naval Architect. The advanced knowledge gained from his JPL experience would nicely replace mentoring in sailboat design.

How Orbital Mechanics is Relevant to You and Your Career

Some long-term career management concepts to consider:

- **You don't have unlimited fuel (time) to accomplish your career mission.**
- **Stay in one orbit too long, and you'll likely be pulled inextricably toward two foregone conclusions: 1) typecasting as a member of that industry or organization, and 2) achievement below your highest level of personal development.**
- **If you stay in orbit for an extended time, choose it because it is part of your "mission architecture."** In other words, make sure that the choice is intentional as part of your greater career journey. While there, be sure to learn that which will facilitate success in getting to your next destination.
- **Have a sense of what characterizes your emerging destination and passion, and be flexible.** Hold a mental

map of your career space, but don't get fixated on only one location as a landing place or one route to get there.

- **Use every work opportunity as a source of energy and learning, not as a final destination.**
- **The type of work (just like planets) that can give you an energy boost isn't available everywhere, nor is it just waiting to beckon you.** You have to predict its location so as to aim for it. Once you've found energizing work, astutely use it as a slingshot towards your next move.
- **Use each round of employment to sling or propel you towards work that is already on your career radar— but be willing to consider opportunities you didn't previously see as part of your route.**

Four Sources of Change That Trigger Career Questions

You'll be asking crucial questions about your career multiple times throughout your life. You'll ask The Three Career Questions at times that may differ from when other people are asking them— even those who are very similar in age, education, or even personality. *There is no scheduled or "correct" time to question your career, but there are more likely times than others based on the amount and sources of change impacting you and your work.*

The Three Career Questions are critical in importance and cyclical in nature. They will reappear throughout your career—but not because you "just can't get it right." They will re-emerge due to the growth, decline, or changes that happen at four different levels of your work experience. Let's examine the four sources of change and examples of what the impact might look like:

1. **Personal Source of Change**. Who are you becoming? You took a job or started a business based on who you were at that time, and now you've evolved, partially as a result of

your last choice of work. The key concept to recognize here is that you are constantly *becoming you*—not "about to become the real you," "almost you," "close to discovering the real you,"...etc. You will never finally *become you* and transform into a past-tense-character in your own history. **Your work needs to evolve along with you.**

EXAMPLE: Some personal inspirations for career changes: You just had a baby? Promoted to overseas location? Stock market just ate 30 percent of your retirement funds? Cancer diagnosis? Hip implant? Selected as a member of the US Olympic team? If one of these scenarios rings true for you, chances are good that your career path and strategy just got a very personal mandate for revision.

2. **Change at Job or Functional Level of the Organization**. The need for your job may be changing, forcing changes in your job function. Look at the number of IT and web-related jobs employing people today that didn't exist five years ago—or machine operator jobs that existed for generations but now are gone from the US work culture.

EXAMPLES: 1) You used to be a German translator, and now software does most of the work. You just review and edit computer output. As a result, you've lost the love of the work. **Or** 2) Your company is growing due to a market shift, and your human resources work (especially recruiting) is becoming more prominent and growing as the organization adds fifteen hundred new employees in seven states. The career questions are quite different for these two professionals.

3. **Organizational Source of Change**. The structure of your organization may be changing, forcing changes in your job function.

EXAMPLES: 1) Your company has been acquired, and your job probably will be eliminated because it is redundant in the new, combined organization. The new merged company only needs one CFO. **Or** 2) More positively, it could be that your company just acquired another firm, and you've been chosen to head up the combined sales forces. It's a promotion for you and a chance to learn management and leadership skills with a larger-than-ever team. For either, it's a big change.

4. **Marketplace Source of Change (Local, Regional, and Global)**. The market around you may be changing.

EXAMPLES: 1) The dollar has devalued to the point that foreign customers are able to buy more of your products or services than ever before. Your role in finance is not only secure now, but you'll also be getting a chance to learn about foreign currency exchange and probably getting a decent raise for the first time in two years. **And/Or** 2) That same currency exchange has crippled your company's ability to buy raw materials for two of the products that your division manufactures. Your role in design engineering may go away, but your current experience and skill in manufacturing will enable you to move to a new division and work at a slightly lower level in manufacturing—probably re-emerging with new skills in the area of robotics.

Right Question at the Right Time?

If you mindfully recognize and monitor these four sources of change, you'll become more likely to consider The Three Career Questions in a timely fashion. But are you asking the *right question* and at the *right time*? This is an important assessment that must be made early in each career strategy discussion throughout your life. Get stuck on the wrong question (even if colleagues around you may be focused on it), and you will waste valuable time and resources developing an action response that doesn't fit you or your situation. An interesting and annoying concept you'll notice is that, if you are pursuing the wrong question, your proposed answer seldom feels compelling. If you are not asking the right question, you'll find that the answers or input you receive never quite motivates you to action and never gets much traction in discussions with people who know you. This "off" feeling may constitute intuition at work, tapping the brakes and saying, "Pay attention to what's *not* happening here."

Case Study
A Lawyer Asking the Wrong Question? It Happens.

Brian's PCT had always been about being a highly-paid lawyer. He had been practicing law in a large private firm since he had left law school thirteen years ago, but now, he really thought he was done with lawyering. The routine of contracts, working in relative isolation on document reviews, and the tyranny of the billable hour had convinced him that he needed to get out of the legal profession. Before accepting this as a foregone conclusion, I asked Brian to describe the various personal interests that occupied his time and the other occupations or businesses he had contemplated.

He was an active parent—taking a genuine interest in teaching his kids about the value of money, both in terms of how to earn it and how to use it. Brian had discussed, with a friend in the software business, the possibility of designing an educational software product that would facilitate children and parents participating in discussions as well as exercises about money and its use. But jumping into the software business with no experience and two small children was not a reasonable risk—no matter how clever he thought his product idea was.

During one of our discussions about his key personal values (which we will discuss later in the book) that were underutilized in his current legal role, Brian described how much he preferred educating and helping as opposed to the arguing or negotiating he did in many of his legal engagements. I asked him if he had ever considered moving into the legal arena of trusts and wills—helping individuals and families learn about and plan for what to do with their money and property, and how to consider family members they wanted to support with their legacies.

As luck would have it, the firm's partner in wills and trusts was retiring in four months; this would create an entry position along with a four-month window to learn the new work without leaving the firm—much less the field of law. Brian's stress levels dropped and satisfaction levels rose as he realized that he was becoming more of who he was meant to be and could now fully participate in his daily work.

How long will Brian's satisfaction last? Probably not forever. Do I think Brian will retire with the firm as the senior partner in wills and trusts? No. But I know he is now able to explore his skills and values in the areas of teaching and helping, and determine their real and practical importance to him—not just their abstract and intellectual importance. That process and outcome will enable him to ask and answer The Three Career Questions even more astutely the next time they cycle around.

The *Career Self-Reliant* person is scanning his or her work situation, monitoring the four sources of change, and asking lots of questions about each source. How do others see these sources of change trending? It's never the wrong time to inquire about change or pending change. The Career Self-Reliant person is taking responsibility for monitoring the ever-changing market conditions and composing career strategies to anticipate those changes.

Key Term

Career Self-Reliance is the ability to manage one's relationship to work in a rapidly-changing environment: the attitude of being self-employed, whether inside or outside of an organization (Career Action Center, Palo Alto, California).

Career Stages and Career Cycles

Stages of growth are an interesting phenomenon to study. Ever notice how you just can't teach a four-year-old to master algebra or negotiate a written agreement with another kid vying for the same piece of playground equipment? Complex numerical reasoning and negotiating skills are not yet feasible within a four-year-old's brain. Similarly, have you ever noticed how a really intelligent, well-educated but inexperienced twenty-two-year-old labor relations intern is not yet able to develop the rapport necessary to be trusted by most of the senior labor reps during contract negotiations? These two examples illustrate that **in order to be fully effective in life or a career, you need more just than intellectual development.**

If we return to the four-year-old and the young labor relations intern after they've added another ten years of mental *and emotional* maturing, however, we might witness some skilled algebra and labor negotiations. Careers develop through some predictable stages in our Western work culture. But unlike human development, these career stages are best understood when unattached to age or biology.

Some career-stage models are based on age or stages of values development. Instead of adhering to these models, I want to present a simple development model that is less dependent on chronological age and more dependent on creating success and satisfaction at any age or career stage.

So many of our models based on age are being overturned today.

The times demand so much change and innovation that rule-busting examples of career moves outside the traditional models abound. Consider these examples:

- **A forty-five-year-old mother returns, after seventeen years of parenting, to seek an MBA in healthcare management.** She learns business norms in a classroom next to a twenty-three-year-old who is competing with the equivalent of "his mother" for good grades and early management roles in the marketplace. The old, chronological models of development wouldn't have predicted this scenario.

- **Our previous example, the fifty-year-old father of two, who can't ignore his passion for flight and sailing, returns to get a master's degree in aeronautical engineering and has to compete with twenty-five-year-old math geniuses.** But his first job is with Jet Propulsion Lab in a position that needs his judgment skills as much as science and math skills.

Three interrelated major trends seem to disrupt the tried-and-true models:

1. Globalization gives competitive work to talent in other, lower-wage-earning countries.

2. Technology is increasingly able to accomplish work that involves decision making, measurement, and judgment calls that only humans made in the past.

3. Innovation constantly changes the nature of work within many occupations and positions (such as web designers, cell phone application developers, orthopedic surgeons).

The result: people may need to change careers more often or at least be in an "always-on" career management mode. Fall asleep in the "mission control center of your career", or even just doze off for a couple of years, and you'll find yourself straining to make sense of the new pattern of options that have emerged.

Stay awake, however, and you may find yourself innovating and able to position yourself in a successful and even more satisfying role.

Five-Stage Model of Career Development

What follows is the practical Five-Stage Development Model of Always-On Career Management. Remember, this model is not based on seniority, longevity, or chronological age. You might even go through all five stages a couple of times in your life, depending on how many careers (not jobs) you create for yourself.

Stages

- **Stage 1: Test one's training with various types of work.** The classical example of this stage is the new high school, trade school, or college graduate who emerges into the job market for a first serious, full-time job. But this may also be the stage experienced by the thirty-year-old with a BS in mechanical engineering who is stepping out with a new master's degree in robotics. He has been working at a metal fabrication firm and wants more technical challenge, perhaps at a local aerospace parts manufacturing operation. Or, this could be the stage of a forty-one-year-old history teacher who leaves education to attend law school and begin practicing law.

  Crucial Career Questions These People Might Be Asking: Is it time to Move Out (for example, of metal fabrication)? Have I been naïve about this occupation? Does this work really fit me? Does my training adequately prepare me for the **real** *work in this industry? How can I adapt my approach to the work so that I earn even more responsibility and access to more significant work? Do I like the people and work at the next level? What specialty within this area of work suits my strengths and would be a good niche for me to develop?*

- **Stage 2: Develop a specialty and reputation within a functional business area.** This is where a well-constructed career strategy starts to pay off. Your work in Stage I gave you a chance to know what you do best and enjoy most—a chance to stake out a type of work on which you can build a reputation. In Stage II, reputation will start to count for a lot more than further content knowledge (education) and technical skill (training). Now, you have to build your reputation with noteworthy specialization in work that produces superior results.

  Our robotics engineering professional demonstrates precision and is trusted to work on jet engine parts and fittings where accuracy and quality are crucial. He also demonstrates an ability to rapidly understand the work of other skilled workers and develops relationships easily around the design shop.

  Frank, our history teacher, becomes a lawyer. He gets to use his gifts, developed while a high school teacher, of showing both empathy and insight with parents. He becomes the family law and mediation specialist in the law firm that hires him after his "experiment" in corporate law (not a good fit).

  How the Questions Might Sound at This Stage: Am I ready to lead others who do this work? Is managing as interesting as doing this specialty function that I've developed? What would the work look like at the next deeper level of functional specialty? Has my education and experience fulfilled my expectations for finding satisfying work to the extent that I should stay in this niche? Am I sought after for advice and my perspective on increasingly complex problems? Does the leadership ask me to lead small task forces or committees for short-term objectives?

- **Stage 3: Take leadership roles based on one's specialty. When is it time to Move Up?** Leadership may or may not constitute a "management job." A chemist may be a thought leader; she designs outstanding research to advance knowledge of cancer cells, but she is not the lab business manager, nor does she supervise other chemists or the lab techs. She leads the research design process.

Sophia, a manufacturing supervisor, loves volunteering for international assignments where she sets up training in new factories being opened in Europe or Central America. One day, she's offered a developmental step up. The manufacturing function needs her to be a training manager and hire two trainers to more rapidly expand the work she has been doing.

Let's also look back at our attorney, Frank. The firm has grown, and he has been there for three years. The management committee that leads the firm's administration and strategy needs to expand. He is invited to throw his hat in the ring for a job on that committee, and he gets it. His appointment to the committee moves him into an additional career beyond being an attorney: he's a manager. This is a profession for which he has never formally trained nor prepared. Has he been Peter Principled (advanced to his level of incompetence)? Did he have a development plan? Was he composing a new narrative about himself as he was doing his regular work? If not, he may feel a bit disjointed or "not himself" as he learns his new role of manager.

How the Questions Might Sound at This Stage: How do I feel about focusing on the productivity of others more than my own service or production activity? Does others' productivity interest me to the point that I want to consider management as my new skill area? Have I started toward another career called "management"? How do I remain **friendly** without being **friends** with the people who report to me? How can I get more scope of authority to correct processes that need adjustment?

- **Stage 4: Lead more complexity and/or scope of responsibility...OR...consider returning to a functional contributor role.** It turns out that our manufacturing supervisor, Sophia, became a training manager and really didn't do well. She failed to address one of The Three Career Questions: *when is it time to Adapt Your Style?* She paid too much attention to the details of the courses her trainers were presenting (her old job) and didn't develop the training function or her role as manager within this new department. Coaching would have helped her adapt her style to participate at a higher level in management meetings and develop her staff (who turned over in the first eight months) instead of micromanaging them.

  Consider the example of Beth. She had moved from quality control/engineering to sales and then sales management. For three years, she achieved outstanding results in her Los Angeles territory. Her next "Move Up" was to manage more complexity, and it entailed adding two additional product lines to her own sales portfolio as well as preparing three new sales reps. Her success with this added complexity led to solid sales results (and a substantial bonus), an eventual addition of three new sales professionals to her staff, and a seat at the next corporate strategic planning meeting.

  How the Questions Might Sound at This Stage: Can I add other functions to my area of oversight and responsibility? How do I influence leaders in functional areas outside of my area (such as human resources). What are best practices that I should develop within these groups? Is this more administrative work than I can tolerate? How can I learn more about our competition? How could we refocus the company at a strategic level rather than just implementing best practices in my functional areas of responsibility? Am I losing touch with the "art and science" of the work I used to love?

- **Stage 5: Move Up again or consider changing to a new...**
  - **Opportunity (job)**
  - **Employer**
  - **Industry**
  - **Function**
  - **Profession**

Beth is working in a technology-driven industry that is most obviously an "up or out" kind of world. The attitude of "up or out" is more common in a range of businesses and even public service jobs wherein the organizations struggle to adapt to a blistering pace of change in markets or political issues. Employees who can't or won't up their games become an increasing burden to other employees' attempts to adapt and innovate. Moving Up traditionally means getting promoted to a higher title and salary. But it can also mean Moving Up to a higher level of self-actualization and results-delivery within a current role.

Beth Moved Up in the classic sense by agreeing to take over the management of the marketing director and his department while fulfilling her current sales leadership role. She was given a new title—VP of Sales and Marketing—which demonstrated a classic development path of promotions.

But let's look at Frank's story. His experience on the management committee of his law firm grew to be incongruent with his values, and the role was not altogether a great match for his limited skills in managing budgets. By participating on the management committee, he replaced some of the tyranny of the billable hour with the tyranny of the law partners' profit motives—which were substantially more aggressive than his. Frank's decision, when faced with this unappealing situation, was as follows: change both industry and job. He became a family court judge and moved into the public sector to complete his law career; by returning to the public employee tribe he was returning to the values he had lived by when starting his career as a teacher. While he didn't take a step up in rank within the firm, he did Move Up to a more complex role of judge.

How the Questions Might Sound at This Stage: Where would I like to show up on the succession plan for this company? Do I want to consider inquiries from recruiters about moving to a new company? Who are the talents coming up behind me to run this organization, and how can I ensure or mentor their capability? How do I balance the competing interests of the corporate functions and the production units? How can my agency lead or collaborate with others in the greater social services sector within this county?

You may only cycle through the Five Stages once in your life. You probably have a family elder who had a classic rise within a single profession or company. The WWII and Boomer generations hold numerous examples of people who progressed through these stages within one large organization—like a metropolitan school district; The Department of Justice; or a company like Intel, Hartford Insurance Company, GE, McKinsey & Company, or a host of impressive and diverse organizations.

But you're more likely to know someone whose career experienced a "reset" during one of the Five Stages and went back to one of the previous stages—including back to Stage 1. Take our forty-five-year-old mother returning to work by way of an MBA program. She will have to "test her training with various types of work" as she exits the program with lots of knowledge but little contemporary experience.

The Three Career Questions operate as an internal gyroscope within *each* stage of your career. As the stages come and go, you inevitably will need to ask and answer The Three Career Questions *more than once.* In addition, the Questions will keep you aware and conscious of your place within each stage and enable you to anticipate and make the best next move.

PART II:

USING THE THREE CAREER QUESTIONS

CHAPTER 3:

WHEN IS IT TIME TO MOVE UP?

"Up"…As in Up the Developmental Curve

Think of the phrase "Moving Up" as representing the developmental curve or forward progress of your career. It doesn't cover only promotion to a higher level of compensation or organization status. It could also mean:

- Moving laterally or down in an organization to get access to work that takes you to your personal next level of development (regardless of what the organization considers "next" to be);
- Developing in place and enriching in the job you've got;
- Changing geographic location to increase the amount of experience you gain.

Case Study
Down, Over, and Up

Mark is coming to terms with being a "career space probe" while he pursues his development strategy. He launched a multi-year "career space mission" within the solar system of a large healthcare organization where he had worked for years. This mission included visits to a couple of minor planets before landing on his target destination, "Planet CEO," a job of a life-time, and in his choice city too. Here's a figure representing his flight plan:

Mark had progressed within the corporate headquarters finance function at a large, regional hospital chain and, in so doing, developed a personal career "map of the hospital solar system" along with a goal of reaching the position of CEO in a San Diego hospital (his dream city). He planned to use orbital mechanics (see Chapter 2) to swing by two other developmental roles and pick up experiential energy and credibility to slingshot him to the CEO role.

4 ... 3 ... 2 ... 1 ... ignition ... lift-off ... er ... life-down ... or, uh over? Wait a minute, how does this work?

1. **First, Down.** The hospital was adapting to a new enterprise resource planning (ERP) platform that would revolutionize the way things were bought, accounted for, and managed throughout the hospital chain. He volunteered to leave a high-level corporate finance role to dive right into the middle of that project as a project manager for eighteen months. This was his first orbital mechanics move; moving down the hierarchy from a prestigious corporate role and picking up crucial energy for the ride toward "Planet Hospital CEO" by first acquiring change management and IT skills—which he would need for the future.

2. **Then, Over.** After leading a successful implementation of the ERP system at a recently acquired mid-sized hospital, Mark asked to transfer over to a larger, long-established hospital within the chain's system. It would be this hospital's turn to roll out the new resource planning system. There, in his second use of orbital mechanics, he applied for the position of VP of administration, touting his capacity to help implement this complex new planning system that was going system-wide over the next year. It worked.

While in this new VP role, the facility benefited from his previously-acquired ERP system implementation and leadership experience (the gravitational energy boost acquired from "Planet Project Manager"), and he picked up energy and credibility as an operational hospital executive. He was officially out of the orbit of Planet Corporate Staff and hurtling his way, using the boosts from new roles, toward Planet Hospital CEO.

3. **Finally, Up.** Finally, the more classic "up" move arrived: a promotion to CEO at the two-hundred-eighty-bed flagship hospital in San Diego. Looking back at his strategic moves, it didn't really surprise Mark, or many other people around him, that he made it to this position. *Pleased*, yes. *Surprised*, no. He was picking up added capability and credibility from each work experience whose "gravity field" he encountered. His moves were thoughtful and strategically well-timed. Each move saw him acting in a Career Self-Reliant manner—actively managing his work life as if he were self-employed and marketing himself to his current employer using skills and actions that resembled marketing his capacities as if he were a consultant or contractor.

Progress versus promotion? Is that a distinction you've made before? Our work culture is evolving *away from* rewarding those who merely know how to make things—controlling their production—and evolving *toward* rewarding those who create or innovate with their knowledge. This shift is moving us from large numbers of formal production organizations that had structure—and status associated with that structure—to smaller, nimbler, knowledge-worker cultures and organizations. Here, talent develops more individually than it does with traditional organizational timelines or definitions of status. So moving "up" now means something different than it once did.

Write Now Exercise
Your Personal "Move Up"

Take a minute to think of your own potential "Move Up." You don't have to do anything about these thoughts right now. Just imagine a move or two that could develop you. Who might you work for or partner with on a project? What is a type of work or position of responsibility that would feel significant and satisfying to you? Write your thoughts in the margins. These are your observations and ideas (not "have to dos") that you need to harvest from your conscious thought right now as you're having them, so that you can return to these brilliant observations and transform them into a future space mission in service of your own development and satisfaction.

Actualization: "Why Not Take All of Me?"

Think of Moving Up and progressing as a form of "actualization," as Abraham Maslow described it in his classic work, *Motivation and Personality* (1970). Let's think of actualization as *the coming to know and express, over a lifetime, all the capacities and talents we have* (my interpretation). Maslow's theory of motivation also suggests that we are drawn to additional levels of personal actualization by the satisfaction of one level and the ensuing hunger or striving for the next level. **We get to experience and release the capacities that are within us as well as develop new ones.** Sound a bit like the cycle of career management driven by The Three Career Questions?

There is some debate over Maslow's theories, so don't get hung up on the research that validates or invalidates them on a technical basis. Instead, let's look at self-actualization as a model that could help us frame what is going on when we Move Up in our careers. First, take a look at the following personal characteristics and ask yourself: "Would I want to work with or for a person with any or all of these fifteen characteristics?"

1. Holds an efficient perception of reality and comfortable relations with it
2. Demonstrates acceptance (of self, others, nature)
3. Values spontaneity, simplicity, naturalness
4. Uses a problem-centered (as opposed to ego-centered) approach
5. Exhibits detachment and the need for privacy
6. Fosters autonomy and independence of culture and environment
7. Shows continued appreciation
8. Has mystic and peak experiences
9. Has a feeling of kinship with others
10. Experiences deep and profound interpersonal relations
11. Values and exhibits the democratic character structure
12. Discriminates between means and ends, between good and evil
13. Has a philosophical, un-hostile sense of humor
14. Respects self-actualizing creativity
15. Resists being totally identified with the transcendence of any particular culture

Working with a person who is like this would be a pretty easy choice to make. These are the characteristics Maslow attributed to self-actualizers. The scarier question is, "Do I work with people like this right now?" You likely feel some of the current tensions at work melt away as you imagine your boss or work group having these self-actualizing tendencies (versus the ones they have now).

So Moving Up also means embodying "actualization," not just

"getting promoted." Let's look at the way moving in other directions could help you accomplish your career objectives while also representing development. In our example, Mark (the hospital CEO) moved down, over, and up. But two other types of moves also can leverage you to a higher level of personal and professional development or progression by actualizing important parts of you.

Case Study
Enriching the Job You Have

Herb had been a career management consultant with a global outplacement firm for more than six years. He had substantially mastered the work of career consultant—as well as the tools, processes, and consulting skills—and was starting to ask himself The Three Career Questions. Specifically, he was asking, *"When is it time to Move Out?"* He was wondering, "Do I have to leave to learn something new and energize the work I do?" It turns out that the answer to this question was "not by a long shot." Prior to the outplacement firm, Herb's work involved roles in start-up companies. One crashed and two made great successes. He never lost his entrepreneurial nature, and thus decided to re-engage it to enrich the job he already held.

Within a month, Herb had surveyed the firm's existing clients and uncovered an under-served need: many wanted to explore self-employment and the entrepreneurial path rather than return to corporate employment. He put together a convincing business case for offering this as part of the outplacement firm's service. He subsequently designed and piloted the program to a rousing success and, in so doing, permanently enriched part of his role as the firm's facilitator of entrepreneurship.

Case Study
Changing Location as a Start to Moving Up

Globalization of business has elevated the need for cultural competency, not just functional competency. Tanya recognized this reality within a year of working for her current firm, a business process outsourcing company (BPO) that provided receivable collection services to hospitals with unpaid patient bills. Tanya worked in the call center located in Omaha, Nebraska, and frequently coordinated work production with a sister call center in Mumbai, India. She was clear that one of the key complexities of profitable collections management was assigning the right contracts to the right call center teams.

Tanya was interested in progressing within the BPO industry and leveraging her interest in languages while developing cultural competency. There was only one way to intimately understand the parallel operation in Mumbai: go there and know it personally, not just conceptually or through what she had gained sitting at the end of a teleconference call. She decided to conduct her management role from Mumbai rather than Omaha.

Her two years in India led to an operational sophistication and ability to manage productivity across multiple simultaneous contracts at a level not previously achieved by any manager. Her ability to harness her experience within different work cultures to better manage complexity became the precursor for her promotion: "Welcome back, Tanya. We think you'll like the headquarters office in Sacramento where you can 'call in' to winter in Omaha."

Are You Behind on the Timeline of Life?

Case Study
Late Start—Come From Behind

"Rod, don't think about this question. Just answer it right from your gut: 'Are you behind on the timeline of life?'" His head just whipped around. He was stunned and staring bug-eyed at me. The fact that he was driving at the time made it important that I "un-stun" him.

"I guess that would be a 'Yes,'" I said.

That "timeline of life" question can tap a raw nerve for many, especially if they don't realize they have a sub-conscious timeline that has been abused or ignored. Rod had one, and I had just jabbed it—intentionally. I sensed that some of his career strategy had an un-named pressure behind it, a pressure that could distort or crash a strategy if it remained subconscious.

Rod had married and had children early, and worked a number of "just keep the bills paid" jobs to manage the life-style he and his wife had created. Like in many premature and stressed families and marriages, a divorce and remar-riage followed—along with years of child support payments. So, when all that cloud of the past finally cleared (in his for-ties), Rod was behind on his self-imposed, unacknowledged timeline of life. As a result, he was pressing himself and his spouse pretty hard to catch up.

Now that we had made the timeline of life a conscious part of conversation and consultation, we could test his embed-ded assumptions for rationality and do-ability. Together, we would assess the answer to, "Are you behind on the timeline of life?" as well as the inferences that preceded my formulation of this question. The instantaneous nature of Rod's reaction to this question in many ways demonstrated the intuitive process of jumping to a conclusion. There were likely to be some "shoulds" and "oughts" lurking in his thinking about where he was "supposed to be" on that timeline. **Shoulds and oughts are a great place to start looking for irrational distortions or imposed values from others.**

As it turns out, there are a number of inferences and assumptions that came before Rod subconsciously began to question himself about being behind on the timeline of life. This is where that seemingly obscure branch of philosophy, erotetic logic (the study of questions and language that calls for a reply), actually has some practical value for us.

He first had to posit the notion that there was a timeline— either one of his own construction or one that was prescribed by others. The other implied inference I witnessed (based on his bug-eyed reaction) was his belief that being behind was a pretty bad thing that had to be corrected. It wasn't a natural thing like being short or having green eyes instead of brown. For Rod, this was bad, and it was driving his anxiety which was, in turn, controlling his career strategy.

Rod was also demonstrating what happens when one's Personal Career Theory starts to break down. The story in Rod's head, or his theory about how his career was supposed to progress, was not playing out according to plan. He had sought my help in untangling some of the assumptions that were irrational and causing him undue stress. Rod was realizing that, when one's old theory breaks down, it must be replaced with a new and better one. It operates as a bit of an internal guidance system, just as all values-based stories do, and revision is essential for healthy choice making and staying on course.

It's a compelling question: "Are you behind on the timeline of life?" Its importance can vary at different stages of life. Having your first child, for example, can be so inspiring and overwhelming that nothing else matters—for a while. Inevitably, however, the timeline question kicks back in. With a little digging into your thinking, you realize the timeline question is increasingly compelling because it is driven by some inferences that say things like: "You should be paying for all of your daughter's college tuition and expenses because your parents did that for you." That kind of thinking, if left to its own devices, will drive a sense of anxiety and urgency as one quietly monitors the escalating cost of college tuition.

Write Now Exercise
Are You Behind in the Timeline of Life?

What is your gut-level response to the timeline question? Your partner's response? Start writing notes in the margins, and I mean write them now. Are you behind? Ahead? Right where you want to be? How does your perspective on this question complement or clash with your partner's? It's important to capture your initial impressions that are unfiltered and not yet rationalized. Just write whatever comes to mind at this time.

Contents of Your Personal Development Plan

Actualizing various aspects of your Self will benefit from being intentional and doing a bit of planning. Your plan will focus on different things as you move along the timeline of life. I've been fortunate to work in a couple of organizations during progressive periods of economic growth when development planning was consciously pursued and openly discussed. In one case, the development discussion was held between paired peers during a staff retreat. The focus was blessedly specific and brief, and the results were poignant.

Case Study
A Surprising Development Suggestion Takes Off

During a staff exercise around professional development, I was paired with Alison, who I'd worked with for about five years. This organization was very progressive in terms of staff development. We actually talked about development as a serious staff agenda item during a series of staff meetings. (*Does your organization do that?*)

Alison and I began discussing the strengths and weaknesses that she brought to her role in outplacement consulting. It turned out that she was pretty burned out on one-to-one consulting with executives in transition. Typically, in this firm, her next developmental step would involve program administration; but Alison was weak in administrative detail management. She couldn't see a next step inside the firm. To her, it looked like her next step would probably be "out."

The counter-intuitive suggestion I gave her was to actually embrace the administrative work, not avoid it. We discussed the possibility of a career move into a role that would develop that weak skill—rather than assume she could not do it and, therefore, needed to avoid it. *Was any of this admin work a complex science that resembled brain surgery or abstract algebra?* No. *Had she ever tried program administration and proven herself unfit?* No. *If she found a job elsewhere, would it probably involve administration?* Yes.

So she began a development action plan that resulted in successive levels of program administration and a brief, interim role as branch manager. The organization benefited from retaining her process knowledge and client relationships. She raised her game to a higher level and conquered assumptions that had put a false ceiling on her development within the firm. Good for the firm. Good for Alison.

Personal Development Plans: Why Have One?

A personal development plan is usually a written document that identifies your developmental goals and objectives within a certain organization over a specific period of time—with the identification of the key resources you'll need to pursue that development plan (such as training, coaching, a certification class, etc.)

The purpose of the development plan is to focus your attention. It's not a promise by the organization nor by you to necessarily do anything. It's a statement of intention. It will make you pay selective attention to becoming more vigilant about things you've decided are significant and related to where and how you want to develop. A plan is a way to prioritize your time, energy, and actions so that you know your top priorities and can get to those items first. It doesn't need to identify specifically where you will land. That kind of detail may be a bit presumptuous and may cause you to become obsessed with the end destination—missing needed course corrections along the way. Think of your development plan as a map of the part of the occupational solar system you want to explore, with types of work and organizations clearly identified as possible planets to visit or even reside on but surely planets to leverage for their capacity to offer the boost of a gravitational slingshot. It's clearly more than a list of training classes to take.

A development plan can really benefit from a degree of formality. "Formality" may just involve discussion with a trusted other or writing down your ideas. But—written, discussed, or both—you'll think about development more rigorously when you commit to a process of examining it. You may, ultimately, reject what you initially discussed or wrote down, and that's not a bad thing, nor does it mean the act of examining it was a lost cause. It means you gave it public or conscious exposure and received significant feedback or insight that led to revision.

So, let's take a look at the elements of a thoughtful person's plan for his or her future.

Elements of a Good Personal Development Plan

- **A Good Personal Development Plan Motivates and Energizes You.** Come on, it's supposed to be about your desires, not someone else's prescription for your future. Include things that you like, and you'll be motivated to work on your plan. *A development plan is not a performance improvement plan to get you out of trouble. If you can't find anything that interests you to put on such a plan, there's a good chance you're in the wrong work or organization.*

- **Limited Goals (Two to Four) Biased Toward Action.** *Keep the plan simple.* No plan should itemize all the things you might want to develop or all the parts of yourself that you want to actualize. Instead, rank and prioritize the aspects of your talent that you are ready to develop based on a combination of internal motivation (for income, recognition, affiliation with certain types of colleagues, a satisfying sense of mastery, etc.) and external needs of the market (what capabilities your employer or other industries and organizations are seeking).

What follows is very similar to the SWOT analysis frequently used to analyze a business and its market standing when developing a strategic plan. That's not just a coincidence. Remember, the Career Self-Reliant professional is thinking and acting as a one-person business.

Sample Personal Development Plan

Armand is a thirty-seven-year-old project manager in a West Coast shipyard that conducts big, complex repair projects on ships ranging from stern-wheelers to oil tankers and mine-sweepers. He is looking to become a better people manager and eventually move to a higher level of responsibility with more complex ship repair jobs.

- **Strengths to Leverage and/or Develop.** Leverage my capacity to foster an atmosphere of positive customer service and treat others with consideration and respect. I'd like to expand on that strength and add cross-cultural experience to it by leading the team as a superintendent or assistant superintendent on a ship repair project that involves a foreign owner and/or owner's representative, and I want to do this within the next eight months. I will use Rene as a coach for questions and issues that may arise since he's the most senior superintendent in the yard.

- **Weakness that Matters.** I need to develop more flexibility in responding to priorities and organizational change. My peer's feedback suggests that they seem to experience me as too rigid in this area. I'm assuming that they're reacting to my reluctance to release certain skilled crafts to other projects that are in a crisis. To confirm this idea, I'll have a brief discussion, within the next two weeks, with three of the other PMs and ask for examples of opportunities where I can try to flex more. If we don't agree on when it's appropriate to be flexible, I'll meet with my manager to discuss this and define appropriate (and inappropriate) opportunities to work on being more flexible.

- **Opportunities for Development.** A German-owned, small cruise ship is asking us for a bid on some service. I'll talk to sales and see if I can be helpful right from the beginning of our relationship with this foreign owner and also ask the COO for the superintendent or assistant role on this project. I'll also look into our contracts archives and see what foreign shipping companies come to us on a regular basis for repair services. That way, I can start to anticipate upcoming projects and lobby the COO to be put on one of them.

- **Threats to My Development.** Rene is the best mentor I have and the most likely next person up for retirement in the next two or three years. I need to start with him and ask his advice as to who he'd recommend as an additional mentor.

The world-wide recession is driving down the volume of shipping, and that could mean fewer repair contracts if companies are too cash-strapped. Or, it could mean more capacity to repair and upgrade ships now that they aren't in service and constantly responding to customer demands. I need to talk to our marketing people and find out more about the trends in this area.

Notice that this Personal Development Plan is not complex or long. But it does focus on action steps that Armand is going to take. He documents these action steps and, if he followed my advice and talked about this plan with a trusted other (a truth-teller, even when it hurts), he should expect that person to follow-up and ask if he'd actually accomplished those actions.

Exploring the Four Parts of Your Development Plan

Let's look at the four parts (SWOT) of your development plan in a little more detail. There are some easy-to-miss aspects to focus on, such as strengths that become weaknesses. You will benefit from some focused attention on this, especially if you've never written one of these plans for yourself.

1. **S** Leverage <u>Strengths</u>

Be clear about your strengths, and leverage them rather than spending a lot of time and energy noticing your weaknesses and trying to eliminate them. It's easier to achieve success by doing more of the things you're good at than by trying to correct all your bad habits or develop all your weaknesses. That being said, see *Address Weaknesses* coming up in the text below.

Strength versus weakness tip: one way to work on a weakness is by doing more of a complementary strength that gets the result you need. See the sidebar for an example.

Case Study
Do More of Something Else Versus Trying to Stop Doing Something

The assessment data confirmed it: Chang is very bright, very outgoing, and intellectually competitive—always wanting to get to the best idea first. Not surprisingly, he suffers from "foot-in-mouth" disease, is prone to interrupting, and does not tend to lead or facilitate others effectively. He's aspiring to management responsibilities beyond his current analyst role, and his coach has made a suggestion for his development.

Given the fundamental nature of his intellect and extroverted interaction with others, he probably couldn't repress those tendencies so as to develop a more facilitative style. Instead, Chang agreed to try using a complementary outgoing behavior that was more natural for him. Specifically, he would practice asking at least two questions of others before offering an idea or solution of his own.

People started noticing that they were actually having interactive conversations with Chang instead of just listening to him fire off hypotheses or suggestions. They felt "heard," even if he didn't agree with them. There was more exchange of information. He started to seem more like someone they could learn from rather than run from.

In terms of management potential, Chang began to develop the ability to do what all successful managers must do: size up the different talents in his team, and know how to astutely match them to the work that best leveraged their strengths. Only by asking more and telling less could this management capacity start to develop in him.

- **Strengths That Become Weaknesses. BEWARE of Achieving to Death.** One of the most compelling quotes from the research literature on leadership development was from the Center for Creative Leadership in Greensboro, North Carolina. It resulted from a study of managers (first conducted in the 1980s, and updated in 1996) that investigated which managers were most able to develop and what characteristics seemed to distinguish their individual development ability.

  When the Center went back to retest the sample of managers in the study, researchers noticed that a surprising number of the participants were gone from their management roles. This became an unexpected and compelling challenge for the researchers to understand. And so, they grew the research project to also be about studying derailers: those characteristics or personal styles that cause a leader's career or work to come off the rails that had been guiding it.

  A summary statement characterized what they found that accounted for much (not all) of the derailments: the demise in their management roles had been caused by "the unchecked use of an unbridled strength." It wasn't lack of education or IQ. It wasn't the training courses they had taken or missed. These derailed managers had taken *something they were good at*—a strength such as quantitative analysis—*that they then over-used without discretion and restraint.*

  This became the unbridled part. For example, they may have used numbers to explain or measure things in financial terms when the issues were related to values or the need for persuasion rather than quantitative proof. *Their behavior was unchecked by feedback or coaching because they had set up a feedback-poor environment around themselves.* They had no truth-teller or trusted source (someone capable and ready to express disappointment, if earned) to say things like, "You know, in that last staff meeting discussion, you needed to explore some of the ethics issues, not just the balance sheet." Finally, they had no TOLL (Think Out Loud Laboratory) to confidentially discuss concerns they had about how they were doing.

So, one of the resources that will propel your development plan is feedback. How are you going to get it? Waiting for it usually means it will come too late. You may get rave reviews about something you already know is good. That won't help. Or, you may get negative feedback in your warning notice or layoff meeting when it's too late to Adapt Your Style and stay on the team.

I'll give additional attention to the need for a feedback-rich environment in Chapter 5 when we consider the third question: *when is it time to Adapt Your Style for greater success?* For now, think about the value of feedback as the raw data or clues that you need to:

- Plan ahead for the work of your future that you want to progress into
- Redesign your work approach to experience more success.

Others' feedback and perceptions don't have to be "correct" to be useful. If feedback represents perceptions that exist at all (even if a bit imprecise), you are still responsible for developing a response to them and managing yourself and your relationships to the feedback-givers.

Write Now Exercise
What About That Feedback?

This might not be such a bad time to write a "note to self" about feedback. In the margin note space, jot down the names of the last two people who gave you useful, hard-hitting feedback, and what they said about you. If you can't recall a time when you received this sort of feedback, check into some assessments you might be able to access through your coach—or human resources or training and development functions at work—so that you gain more insight into your strengths. No recent feedback? Write the names of two people you can ask by the end of next month.

---

2. **W** Address **Weaknesses**

We're finally there: at the negative stuff. This is where most people start their development planning, find what's broken, and fix it. Managers who receive feedback from assessments are often prone to over-focusing on the lower scores or critical comments without asking a crucial question, "Does it matter for success at this time?"

You only have limited time and consciousness to spend on various activities, so your choice of time investments better matter. *Don't sweat the small stuff.* Let's look at a few lenses you can look through to view the feedback and see if it matters for success at this time.

- **Personal Lens.** If the feedback is critical of something that is fundamental to your personality (perhaps being introverted or deeply spiritual or motivated by achievement rather than power), you may have a fit problem more than a development issue. Your personality or values may not be ready to change that much, and working against those personal aspects every day by trying to act like someone who is "not you" will create trust and credibility issues on top of the issues you already have. If this is the case, it's time to ask the next crucial question: *when is it time to Move Out?*

- **Job Lens.** Is this the right job for you? Is the job designed in a rational way and achievable, or is it substantially undoable by almost anyone who might attempt it? If there is a fundamental flaw in the job design, or the job is just a poor fit for you, you're development plan will look different than if it's a great job and you're just not quite able to achieve the necessary level of results. A job that is poorly designed or a poor fit for your level of experience or skills will require a lot of development. If the job is unrealistic in its design, you may have an organizational or strategic problem that must be addressed before you dedicate personal time and great energy to meeting those job expectations.

- **Organization/Function Lens.** You may be quite competent at your job, but you're in a functional area (such as sales) of the company that you don't like as well as the last area where you worked (such as marketing). You're able to achieve sales quotas, but you're often quite critical of the sales strategy or values that drive some of the other sales team members. Maybe sales, as it's done here, is work you "can do" but not work you "want to do." The critical feedback you're getting may be due to the fact that others are experiencing you as a non-fit within your current department or functional area. You don't seem to value the same things or approach work with the same style as others.

You may need to examine some of the values necessary for success in this line of work and consider shifting some of your own values. This doesn't mean selling out or becoming disingenuous. It might mean putting a higher value on working independently within your sales territory versus adhering to the way things were done as a team in your previous marketing department. Nobody is wrong and nobody is right here. It's about values that drive certain teams or functions within an organization. **Fitting in without selling out matters.** If you value the work and the experience, don't forget to consider flexing to adapt and develop your work style to accommodate your current tribe. (Question #3, When is it time to adapt your style?)

- **Market Lens**
  - <u>Realize a False Positive.</u> Sometimes feedback may be glowingly positive and yet still be associated with a weakness that only becomes clear by viewing the feedback through the market lens. Let's say you've received praise and reinforcement for three great quarters of growth in your sales figures, and you've decided to leave this position and apply for a higher-paying sales position in a high-risk/high-reward start-up company. First, let's look at the market context for a reality check.

    There is a bull market on Wall Street. A boom economy is flush with cash, and it's being spent with much more lenient hands on the corporate purse strings. And you had three good quarters. Well, who didn't, in a market like this? **If you haven't perfected your sales skills by working in both good and bad markets, you may be a bit more mediocre, or at least untested, than your current feedback would suggest.**

    This scenario played out for many at the end of the dot.com boom. Young managers supervised inexperienced salespeople who were selling anything in a boom economy market, but neither had the experience to see the end coming. When the dot.bomb finally imploded, many were shocked that their spiffy sales records during the boom didn't translate to a lot of credibility during the downturn.

- Benign Goes to Critical. You may notice your feedback has changed from benign to critical with your boss, but stayed positive with your peers. Hmmm, let's take a look at your boss's PINT (Problems, Issues, Needs, and Trends) that matter TO HER at this time—before we declare her feedback inaccurate or not. (More about how to use a PINT Analysis in Chapter 4: "When Is It Time to Move Out?")

  Your company is distributing auto products, and the market is terrible and getting worse. Your boss is under pressure to create higher levels of sales, innovation, cost savings, and efficiencies and, what a surprise, she's passing that pressure on to you and your co-workers. If your market was booming, there is an equally likely chance of getting upbeat feedback due to market conditions that you didn't create and for which you can't take credit. But you would probably accept the positive feedback and bonus check from your boss nonetheless.

- **Weaknesses That Suddenly Matter.** Review the sidebar case study to see how it might look as former skills or behaviors that were positive, or at least inconsequential, start to be seen as detrimental—and the negative perceptions of others start to sneak up on you.

Case Study
The Stealth Attack on Your Career

For years, Rajit had been able to lead with a style that was interpersonally skilled and outgoing and involved spending time with direct reports, going to lunch with them, and hosting special training or design-critique sessions in the conference room. His reputation got him noticed, and he was even asked to manage a remote team located twelve hundred miles from his office.

Over the years, Rajit had received so much good feedback as a leader. That's why he literally didn't know what to do when he got feedback from a leadership 360 assessment that described a number of direct reports experiencing his style as "impersonal, stingy with feedback, and unable to create strong followership or set a clear vision."

What happened? How could he suddenly become weak at such a proven set of skills?

He didn't suddenly become weak. A weakness that was already there but seemed insignificant suddenly emerged, and it was critical for success at this time in his expanded role. Rajit's ability to manage staff at a distance with the skillful use of communication technology tools was something that he never needed until he was given responsibility for the struggling office of thirty-five employees located twelve hundred miles away in another part of the country. Rather than improve his understanding of and skill with these technology tools, he continued to rely only on his interpersonal leadership style with the remote office—that he practically never visited. Consequently, the remote employees seldom *saw* his strongest leadership style because Rajit was seldom with them in person. They never saw the reason to trust him as a leader and therefore found his leadership and vision to be insubstantial in their daily work experience.

These "stealth attacks" don't have to be fatal. The key is to create a feedback-rich environment for yourself that provides you with frequent updates about how you're doing before anything negative gets too big or serious.

3. O Identify <u>Opportunities</u>

Now comes the part for which the Personal Development Plan is most necessary. We've looked inward at your strengths and weaknesses and decided what to do with them. Now, we must look outward. At this time, you need to apply your insights about yourself and identify actions and opportunities that will leverage your strengths and develop the weaknesses that matter for success. A Personal Development Plan creates a vigilance about what development resources you're looking for and helps you spot them more readily in the otherwise cluttered field of vision that is everyday work life.

Let's go back to Alison (the consultant at the outplacement business) and her counter-intuitive realization that embracing more administrative duties would cause her to learn critical skills—while giving her access to different and more interesting long-term work. Because she consciously committed to that goal, and made the commitment out loud to me, she was very alert to opportunities to volunteer taking on administrative challenges.

When the implementation of a new service program came down from corporate, she shifted away from her old pattern of avoiding all things corporate and stepped up to volunteer. Yes, there were some raised eyebrows and puzzled looks. And no, she didn't do a perfect job on this first challenge. But others pitched in to help, gave honest feedback, and were grateful for her efforts. This on-the-job, action learning was developmentally crucial to Alison. It was the kind of action learning that developed and demonstrated her capabilities while enabling her to temporarily fill in as an interim branch manager a year later.

- **Types of Opportunities to Seek.** Do not limit your own development by thinking that it comes primarily in the form of training or academic classes. Most leadership development is accomplished through challenging field assignments or even failures. That works for leadership development, but I'm not proposing the same sort of learning style for neurosurgeons, nuclear reactor directors, or airline pilots. Not by coincidence, certain professions require a lot of classroom education and controlled simulation training.

  Because most of us don't work under life-and-death circumstances, however, our industries have cut back on formal training for many types of skills. *Consequently, you're going to have to look for development opportunities in various forms.*

- **Development Opportunities May Include:**
  - A stretch assignment that will challenge you to learn on the job. It also will require that you be conscious and specific about extracting the lessons you learned;
  - A role model who you can watch;
  - A sponsor who will guide your candidacy for a new role by getting you assigned to the most appropriate work or committees;
  - A mentor who can share the story of his or her path as well as insight into the types of circumstances that favor or hinder success;
  - A coach who can help you craft behavioral strategies for success and harvest insights along the way.
  - PROBLEMS that need solving; something that's broken (process, team, or relationship) that you can fix;
  - ISSUES that need addressing; something that needs thought, analysis, and innovative ideas (it's not broken, but it needs attention—such as a regulation or law that changes the way you conduct business);

- NEEDS to be filled; an unfilled need for knowledge, ability, time, leadership, or diplomacy;
- TRENDS that your organization needs to take advantage of; new market scenarios are emerging, and the organization needs help positioning itself (through marketing, public or government relations, advertising, new product design, or old product elimination);
- Something (a product, office, new division of the organization, or campaign) that needs to be designed and built from scratch—that you can launch or help create;
- A switch from working in a production or service area of the company to working in a corporate role (or the reverse).

Write Now Exercise
Your Strengths, Weaknesses, and Opportunities Analysis

Write now would be a good time to jog on over to the margins and describe a few types of ideal opportunities that would leverage your strengths or develop weaknesses that have come to matter at this time in your work.

Key: Keep it simple. Write:

- Two strengths and a type of opportunity that would increase them;
- One weakness that matters now and a type of opportunity that could help you improve it;
- Write the name of one person that could help you in any way.

Later, you can return and find these thoughts and suggestions-to-self to guide your next actions.

Ideal, real opportunities to develop can come in the form of:

- People
- Places
- Training
- Academic classes
- Challenging assignments and even mistakes that happen during a challenge

But you have to both create them and spot them in the environment around you. Nothing sharpens your vision like a plan and a commitment to self and others to pursue the plan. Development planning is a good place to use your truth-teller resources (calling on that someone you have identified who is capable and ready to express disappointment if you don't follow through on your plan).

4. **T** **State Your Response to Development <u>Threats</u> Versus Just Noticing the Impacts of Threats to Your Development**

Another part of your plan should be an assessment of threats to your development that come from the condition of your boss, organization or your market. If these are in transition due to growth or decline, it may mean that the need for certain talents are rising or falling. This is when you have to know which of your talents should be in play to provide crucial value to your target organization or current employer. Then, you have to position that crucial aspect of your talent so that others can notice and employ it. Never assume others have accurate or complete knowledge of your talent.

In 2009 to 2010, the auto industry went into a worldwide decline and reorganization. If you were an astute mechanical engineer, designer, or sales professional, you saw this coming and started your PINT (Problems, Issues, Needs, and Trends) analysis and a focused inquiry into other related markets and their talent needs. (More about how to use a PINT Analysis in Chapter 4: "When Is It Time to Move Out?")

Perhaps you noticed, for example, that Oregon is a growing center of excellence—attracting investment and expertise related to electric vehicles, battery systems, alternative fuels, and solar power generation. You assessed your talents that were transferable to the needs of these industries, and you positioned those aspects of yourself to become more visible to people in these industries. You were thinking like a Career Self-Reliant entrepreneur. You were focused on your response, not just on the impact of this negative market trend on your current employment.

The other type of "threat" within your industry and to your career can actually come from growth. Let's say your firm has decided that growth by acquisition is the only way to maximize existing sunk costs and systems and to increase profitability (not just revenue). The organization will need managers from your level who can take over acquired firms, manage a balance sheet, and substantially run the business. By the way, they'll also want these managers to be geographically flexible and ready to move in a heartbeat.

If you're response is, "I'm ready to move," then the organization's new business strategy isn't threatening your career—but rather offering developmental experiences. But, let's say your wife just got promoted to partner in an accounting firm, and you have two kids in high school. You have a potential mutiny on your hands if you even suggest moving to Salt Lake City. You just got a blow to your job and career even though it started with growth of your business—something we've come to think of as positive. Your threat analysis (SWOT-strengths, weakness, opportunity, and *threats*) needed to see all things—you, the company, your family, and business trends—as systemically connected and capable of influencing each other. Consider "my response" and "what will I DO" instead of just "impact on me."

"Thinking response versus just calculating impact" requires having contingencies, stories, mental movies, scenarios, game plans, and fantasies about actions you can take in response to these systemic changes around you. Many people (especially extroverted types who are known to "think with their mouths open") don't thoroughly understand their own plans and hopes until they compose them and say them out loud. That's where the real awareness, analysis, and learning begins. The first plan or statement of intent is often not the final one. It has to be shaped and reworked a bit.

This is a challenge that benefits from spending time in the Think Out Loud Laboratory. Find the people with whom you can comfortably think out loud, and begin the process of stating out loud your potential responses to change—where trusted others can challenge or complement your ideas.

- **Sources of Feedback.** The last part of your Personal Development Plan needs to include a clear identification of feedback sources that you can and will use in the next twelve months. These sources will provide the feedback and observations necessary to determine if you are making progress on your development actions.

Feedback sources can be formal and quantified, and may include:

- **360-degree feedback** from boss, peers, direct reports, customers, or board members that comes from a research-based or formally created set of assessment questions.
- **A psychological assessment** to determine personality type, values, interest patterns, or various forms of intelligence.
- **Fishbowl exercises.** The fishbowl refers to participation in a discussion, negotiation, problem solving, or other situation while being observed by trainers who make detailed and skilled observations about your behavior and level of skill—measured against training or behavioral standards and/or the outcome of the exercise.

- **Role playing.** Role playing is better referred to as "practice" or "rehearsal." Trainees always complain that, "Role playing is so unrealistic and fake." True, and so is practicing tennis or your Powerpoint presentation before a crucial, upcoming, on-stage experience. But you do it so that you can see, hear, and feel your skills in action—not just think about your tasks in your head.

- **Simulations.** Simulations are designed experiences that imitate the challenge of real work. For example, you might be given a series of decisions to prioritize for presentation during a time-limited meeting. How well you facilitate discussion, the quality of the decisions, and completion of the process within the timeframe are all assessed—and feedback is provided.

Feedback sources also can be qualitative and less formal. You might develop a set of personal style or performance questions for key people to answer anonymously—submitting their answers through a third party (usually someone in a coaching or training role). Or, you may ask someone (such as a boss, peer, or colleague) to give you feedback after a meeting, sales call, presentation, or other business event.

Keep one important criteria in mind when you're choosing sources of feedback: at least one source needs to be your truth-teller...

Someone

  Capable

    And

      Ready to

        Express

          Disappointment in your
          behavior—if you *earned* it.

Note that the point here is not to surround yourself with negative people who are prone to constant disappointment in general or with you. Rather, you need to protect yourself from feedback-givers who are only willing to provide positive or vague feedback. You need a truth-teller who values your development goals to the point that he or she would feel disappointed if you didn't follow through. Additionally, if the truth-teller is to be trusted in expressing his or her real perceptions, he or she must be without conflicting or dual relationships. For example, you wouldn't ask for hard-hitting feedback from a direct report whom you could potentially promote or fire.

Write Now Exercise
Who Can You Ask for Feedback?

Write now would be a good time to jot down the names of three people you need to talk to next week about feedback. These may or may not be the same people you identified earlier as having given you feedback in the past. I'll meet you over in the margins to see who you wrote down and why.

The Saving Grace for Your Development

Your capacity to be a reflexive learner helps to insure your development plan and its strategic chosen activities.

Key Term

Reflexive learning involves having *the habit and skill to look back, assess what you experienced and the lessons learned, and then consciously apply them going forward.*

People who merely accumulate more and more experience don't necessarily learn, nor do they thrive. *They just work really hard.*

Reflexive learning is the saving grace that keeps you from having to learn the same lesson multiple times. This habit of learning followed by reflection supports two of the qualities of a self-actualized personality, which include a:

1. more efficient perception of reality and more comfortable relations with it;
2. continued freshness of appreciation.

Case Study
Sales Lesson

Julie had been through basic sales training and shown herself to be an avid student of the literature and quite good at the in-class exercises, often finishing before her classmates. After finishing a recent class in time-management, she was on the road making sales calls with her boss, Marcus. Something didn't feel right after their last call, but at least they were on time for the next call.

This is when Julie sensed it was time to reflect on the last call and ask her boss for feedback. Having your boss on a sales call can be intimidating, but it may be one of the rare times you get to "reality check" how your sales *Skyle* (combination of skill and style, which we will discuss later) is working. So she asked about how the pacing and time management of the meeting felt to Marcus.

Marcus expressed that he felt the meeting had been pretty good in general, but that Julie had been offered a key piece of relevant, personal information by the client at the end of the meeting and had done nothing to explore it. Yes, the information had come late in the meeting, but Marcus shared that it was essential to discuss such matters while they were current and still "hot."

The two sales professionals began a really good discussion about in-the-moment decision-making required in these ambiguous situations.

Julie learned of ways to start and manage a good meeting agenda that was more likely, in the future, to uncover crucial information at the beginning of the discussion—thereby making time-management a little easier. This valuable new perspective wasn't gained in the class Julie had just completed. It was the product of the reflexive learning and continuous benefit that comes from questioning and discussion after the book is closed and the class is over.

Use a coach or a trusted colleague to debrief your experience and development plans periodically, and I don't mean every five years. Your learning can really increase if you don't keep it all in your own head, but actually apply it to real work or explain and discuss it with someone else. Remember the Tornado from Chapter 1: "Why Questions Instead of Answers?" The Tornado of spinning thoughts and feelings, or lessons learned from development experiences, can be hard to turn into usable insights and action plans. Your debriefing with another person can clarify and simplify your thoughts and learning if you talk about the process. You can often get even more clarity if you write about those experiences and ideas. But spinning them in the Tornado is, well, just about as useful as it sounds.

Development on Your Vacation?

All of your development experiences don't have to take place at work. Within a week prior to going on vacation, go into the TOLL (Think Out Loud Lab) with a colleague or coach and debrief on your development strategy and recent lessons learned. This can look like a coffee conversation, a lunch together, or a brief appointment to "run some ideas by you." This is a conversation with that trusted other person who can hear your ideas about professional development and not be threatened or competitive.

Here's where you can get some provocative and unexpectedly valuable perspectives. Insights and plans from the TOLL can then be further discussed in more relaxed situations with people you meet on your travels. People who are outside your normal scope of interaction are likely to offer you personal stories of success or overcoming adversity, and ideas or introductions that are new and insightful.

Case Study
Trying on a New Work Identity

Olga had discussed her business plan for the first time with her career coach and a close friend just before going on a vacation cruise. It seemed timely and kind of natural because her proposed entrepreneurial business concept related to the travel industry. First, Olga went into the TOLL for thirty minutes with her career coach to show him a brief, written business model and refine some questions about it. The next day, she talked with a close friend about the business—including some of her fears about being economically self-reliant.

Something crucial had started to happen by way of these conversations; an ego relocation process was occurring. Olga was beginning to shift how she thought about and defined herself professionally. She was no longer just an employee of someone else's business, but now a potential creative, risk-taking, rational business woman in the travel industry. Her ego identity was beginning to relocate out of "job mentality" into an entrepreneurial, self-employment mentality.

A funny thing happened on the cruise. She was around a group of intelligent, successful people who she would probably never see again. She could risk revealing her new business identity without freaking out anyone who had become used to thinking of her only as a senior materials developer for Nike, living comfortably in Oregon. So, she announced her new work identity and the business idea to at least eight different people when they asked, "What do you do?" And, the results? She gained:

- An outrageously valuable lead to someone in her targeted sector of the travel industry;
- Advice she would have paid thousands of dollars to get from an attorney or CPA;
- Cautions from a travel agent with fifteen years of experience;
- Encouragement from two people who owned their own businesses;
- Recognition—from people who fit her target customer description—that her idea had potential.

Consider linking your development discussion to your next vacation. You might come home with new enthusiasm for your next career move and a few specific ideas and people to help—in addition to a tan. Whether your career strategy is entrepreneurial or focused on a job search, remember that interacting and doing market research outside of your own local market is a great way to avoid reluctance from knowledgeable, local professionals who feel you might be their future competitor. People from another state will tell you things about their work or business that someone from your own city might feel are a little too competitively sensitive to reveal. And, if you're looking to meet people, it's always best to go on vacation with a question you'd like to answer or a topic of personal interest you'd like to pursue. You can't lose with this idea.

Questions Others Have Asked Themselves

Get a flavor of what kinds of questions others have had at a time in their careers when it was time to Move Up. These questions come from a range of professionals who have attended my classes and workshops, "Three Career Questions You Must Answer...More Than Once," over the last four years. I asked them not only about questions they were asking themselves but also about other recurring thoughts, emotions, and even bodily feelings that they were experiencing during this period in their careers.

Key Questions People Asked Themselves During the Time When They Needed to *Move Up*:

- Am I going to be able to utilize my skill set here?
- Why isn't this fun anymore?
- Why did this challenge me in the past, but not now?
- What's next?
- Where is the "horizon"—the challenge?
- Am I losing ground in this role?
- I want to be a great manager. Is now the right time?
- Am I capable of management responsibility here, or should I move to another organization?
- What is there to learn now?
- Is there a next level available to me in my department?
- Why are we discussing this again? I thought we resolved this issue.
- What are the advancement opportunities?
- Have I learned everything I can from this position?

Thoughts and Feelings at That Time:

- My boss is just looking to repeat the past without innovating.
- I'm so bored.
- My manager keeps missing market signals or opportunities.

- I'm just swirling around in a circle, wasting potential.
- I'm turning my problem solving focus in on myself instead of focusing it on the business.
- Why is this trivial work so important/urgent? There must be something more significant.
- I'm hopeless about my job, but hopeful for the organization and my coworkers.
- I will experience no advancement without a (<u>fill in the blank</u>) degree.

Want More?

Visit www.3questionsconsulting.com to download an extra PDF set of the questionnaires and tools from this book to use for yourself—or to offer to friends and colleagues as they answer The Three Career Questions. See an example of an individual's completed set of questionnaires and the development plan that resulted from the insights he gained.

CHAPTER 4:

WHEN IS IT TIME TO MOVE OUT?

The full question is, "When is it time to Move Out of a job, organization, industry, or profession—once you've already realized that the work or the situation no longer fits?" For professionals who feel either a) confident enough to have their condition improved by competing in the open labor market or b) discouraged enough that they have nothing to lose from pulling the rip cord, this answer comes to them easily. For the rest of us, there is probably reluctance to raise the question at all because it requires changes to many aspects of our lives in addition to work.

My own experience with this question happened under circumstances that were unmistakable and simply had to be addressed.

Pulling the Rip Cord to Find "Me" Again

It was one of the worst recorded cases of industrial-cultural whiplash. And it was self-inflicted. I moved from a high-tech turnaround with lots of fast-moving change and progressive thinking—an organization that was performing on the edge of contemporary organizational development—to a regulated, traditional, electrical utility with organized labor as part of the workforce.

Each day at work was a struggle. I experienced pit-of-the-stomach dread and a sense that I was lifting dead weight that would never come to life or lighten up. I kept having little talks with myself about "trying a little harder...trying again and hoping it would be perceived and received better...trying it another way..."

Then, I decided to try a different thought experiment—a different style of questioning about this dilemma. I decided to fast-forward this bad movie I was starring in. I asked myself a really crucial set of questions: "What if things did get better, and so much better that I got promoted? Would I feel better at that next level up? And would I feel more aligned with the colleagues I'd find there?"

The answers were: "No," and "Noooooo way."

Two of The Three Career Questions came to mind:

1. **When is it time to *Adapt Your Style*?**

    Some of the likely adaptations seemed to require me to be "not me"—in enough ways that I was not interested in trying to answer this question. It seemed a lot like suggesting I switch handedness; I was a "righty," but my current situation was "lefty."

2. **When is it time to *Move Out*?**

    The work and the culture did not fit me, and it was *time to Move Out*. A bold move? Yes, more than one colleague admitted to wishing he or she had the courage to do the same but, they all felt stuck. Scary? Yes, but I was thankful for the experience that taught me when to realize a bad fit with no advantage to hanging on.

The Urge to Delay Moving Out

Many of our colleagues have been conditioned to passively manage their careers by waiting for their managers to suggest a change, promote them, or lay them off. This is part of the Old Guard's story of how careers progress, regress, or change: "Others do it to you. Your exit is caused by your boss, HR, another department, a merger or buyout, or a recession."

For my own situation, I chose an approach that was quite counter cultural. I decided to resign. And I decided to ask for resources to help me make my career move—and make it soon. I turned down an offer to have another job created that would be a better fit. Thanks to the two questions I had deeply contemplated

AND discussed with trusted others (Move Out? Adapt Your Style?), I knew enough not to play it safe and try remaining in work and a culture that didn't fit me or adequately benefit my employer.

An important lesson came from discussing my move with trusted others. Two colleagues revealed to me that they had interviewed for the very job that I had taken. They had both seen landmines and conflicts embedded throughout the organization and the job. Most importantly, they had enough sophistication to walk away from the interviews with a diplomatic, "No, thank you." While this was confirming for my decision, resigning was still an awkward move to announce, and didn't happen without some sense of failure and doubt.

And then, the most shocking thing happened. After I had announced my resignation, a colleague walked into my office, closed the door, and threw her body up against it. Her eyes were filled with tears, and her voice was shaky. What she said next filled me with both sadness and respect for her boldness. "I just want you to know," she said, "that you're doing what I wish I had the courage to do: quit. But no, I'm going to stay here and accumulate even more years of experience that I won't be able to transfer into any company that I really want to work for." And with that, she opened the door and bolted out without another word.

My decision to leave was made in the spirit of Career Self-Reliance. Others may not be so motivated or have the financial savings or local economy that affords them the chance to Move Out when they realize their work doesn't fit them anymore. But, when it is feasible to leave, **there is a price you extract from yourself (and probably your employer) if you stay in the wrong work. The price is your loss of courage and respect, and perhaps the need to rationalize the reasons you didn't leave.** There emerges a need to create some temporary ego protection and a socially acceptable and somewhat true story you can tell others. But there remains, inside yourself, regret and doubt about why you stayed.

This is a time during which I struggled to decide what my new Personal Career Theory was going to be. My old PCT was going to require revisions that I hadn't expected. I had composed a PCT that seemed to include, mostly by default, an ongoing series of corporate jobs that would comprise the story of my career. Now, I found myself in a serious pattern interruption, and I needed to explore what this meant for my future work. I needed to more deeply understand the work that truly motivated me while differentiating it from the things I was merely capable of doing.

Old-Way vs. New-Way of Making Career Changes

Let's take a look at the shift in thinking and behavior that contrasts contemporary, Career Self-Reliant style to the style of a passing era. Keep in mind, there were plenty of rewards and motivations to make the Old Way rational for its time. The following chart will give you a quick (and probably familiar) look at the two mindsets that can drive careers.

OLD WAY	NEW WAY
Passive Receptive	Self-Reliant
Old Guard	Vanguard

- **Event-driven**
  Move Out only if you were laid-off. Move Up after an anniversary date marked sufficient time in position.

- **Job matching**
  Determine your skills and simply match them to the requirements of jobs that are open. Leave your values at the door if you have to.

- **Focus on promotion**
  Try to Move Up, even if that means into a management role that you don't really enjoy.

- **Linear career paths within a specialty**
  Your career moves like a projectile—aiming for a straight-line of upward promotions within the same function, same company, or government agency.

- **Management/HR-driven changes**
  Your boss decides how and when your work should change. Human resources professionals and policies are the planning agents and drivers.

- **Proactive, always-on career strategy**
  Act as if you are self-employed even when working for an organization. Be self-directed as well as interdependent with colleagues.

- **Values and work are aligned**
  Look for match quality with your values, the work that you will do, as well as the organization's operating values (not just the skills or tasks).

- **Focus on learning and personal capacity-building**
  May require moves that are international, lateral, or even down the organizational chain of command.

- **Portfolio careers**
  Includes multiple roles or types of work performed over years and even simultaneously. Orbital mechanics principles are used to harness the learning/energy from each job, staying only for three to five years in any single position.

- **Self-directed/initiated changes (as well as you as employer)**
  This puts you in the role of architect as well as builder of your career. It requires you to always be looking over the horizon to anticipate the PINT (problems, issues, needs, and trends) that impact the work you want to do.

It's not that the Old Way didn't work for a lot of people. But the Old Way became less reliable as employers became more difficult to count on. As companies practiced more and more competitive strategies of outsourcing, downsizing, rightsizing, reorganizations, and mergers, workers of all kinds became less loyal and less likely to expect their needs would be met over time from one employer.

We must factor in another major trend: the move to redefine more and more work as mere projects. This is particularly relevant for products with short product life-cycles. This fact makes it easier, even necessary, to define work as discrete projects that can be outsourced to lower wage labor. The age of the massive and complex US production line—associated with making cars or TVs or washing machines—has long since become industrial history in many companies.

With the rise of rapid change in products and services, as well as the use of projects to define work, the model for careers and how they are managed also has had to change. One can no longer count on staying with an employer for as long as one desires. One of the implications of this for your career management is that some of your sources of information about work need to come from outside your current employer. **If you are laid off or choose to leave on your own, in this new work culture, you need to maintain alternative sources of information about opportunity.** The Passive/Old Way is dangerous. The Self-Reliant/New Way fits the current reality.

It's time we paired up one of the facts of our work culture with the way we manage careers. It has long been understood, since the original research by the Department of Labor, that most of the work now available in our economy is not advertised to the public in the commonly available media (such as newspaper, TV, trade magazines, and even public web listings of jobs). With this reality of our current work culture comes a clear and present danger to any searching talent who passively waits to have opportunity revealed through such public and easily accessed means as a website.

The Career Self-Reliant person is looking out and ahead of himself and constantly refocusing his inquiry into the market. He does this by asking questions about matters that are of genuine interest to him and also related to things he can do with his talent to positively impact these matters in his chosen market. He is constantly uncovering work that needs to be done without relying on others to necessarily go to the trouble to publicize it to job seekers.

Occupational Anti-Gravity (the Layoff) and "You're Gone. You're News."

Unlike planets with gravity fields that attract things, some jobs can push you away. Being laid off is like "occupational anti-gravity." It may seem like a cruel, random, and non-directional, repelling force when it first spits you out. But use it wisely, and you can harness the energy of a layoff for your own mini Big Bang. (I know, I know, "mini" and "big" seem contradictory. Just work with me here.) **Just as galaxies are formed with a Big Bang that spews energy and matter out into the universe, a layoff actually contains energy that you may not have realized.**

When most companies have a downsizing, layoff, right-sizing, reduction in force, slicing the salami (a series of layoffs), or clearing the deadwood (how politically incorrect do you want to get here?), it may make the news. If the company conducts layoffs all the time or only has a small layoff, it may not be big news. But when *you* lose the one job you have, it's BIG NEWS to you and the People-Who-Know-and-Love-You: the inner circle of your network. You've got to use the energy embedded in this newsworthy moment. It's newsworthy because YOU—not just anybody—are gone from your job. There is attentive energy around this moment that needs to be carefully harvested by you—and right away.

Clients have reconfirmed this phenomenon over and over. I recall the first time I was personally caught up in a layoff. Before I had the sense to call out to colleagues, the inbound calls came from people in my inner circle. Then the calls came from people I didn't even think knew where I worked. My network had started to send the alert and mobilize people's energy and curiosity. Other business opportunities started to emerge. Interviews began and, sure enough, an offer was made, which I took. But it was the wrong one to accept. I hadn't really explored my Big Bang of opportunity that might have formed planets of great beauty and creative work opportunity.

As it turned out, I headed for the most convenient planetary body in my solar system of work. And then, I realized before going into permanent orbit that this new work planet had a hostile atmosphere that could not support a healthy work-life for me. So, with orbital mechanics as my guide, I used the brief time within the gravitational pull of the company to slingshot myself toward one of the vendor companies I had contracted with and truly admired. It was a global outplacement firm that gave me a developmental platform for my growth while I helped grow their bottom line.

My career mission and vision sounded something like this: "Make the next move into work that generates revenue and makes a company profitable. Avoid being part of a function that is considered 'overhead.'" You can harness energy of all kinds (attractive or repulsive energy) if you have a vision you're aiming for, and if you consciously try to focus the energy on behalf of your vision.

Now, back to _your_ Big Bang. _Generally speaking, once the word is out about your departure from your last employer, you've got approximately a six-week window of time during which you're departure is newsworthy to your network._ During that time, people will genuinely want to know:

- What happened;
- What you're going to do next;
- How can they be of assistance.

This is the valuable potential energy (others' genuine curiosity) given to you by the occupational anti-gravity that expelled you from your last job. Here's what it can enable you to **do**:

- Enhance your ability to get face-to-face meetings with people.
- Hold people's interest as you talk about lessons learned from the downsizing.
- Mobilize people to think out loud with you about opportunities.
- Motivate people to give you feedback about what they've seen as your strengths.
- Foster people's sense of urgency about taking action to make an introduction on your behalf, find a piece of information you need, or sign a contracting or consulting agreement with you.

Remember, you've got approximately six weeks before the "You're gone; you're news," window closes, and then you're pretty much like every other person who is networking.

When It's Time to Move Out—One Reason to Wait

"The Package." That could be a reason to briefly delay your decision to Move Out. "The package" refers to severance or retention benefits that may be offered to those who are thinking of leaving an organization.

Tyler had developed a career management instinct for using orbital mechanics to accelerate toward organizations, learn from them, contribute to them, and then, with upgraded energy levels (recall the gravity boost planets give to our space vehicle), shoot out of their gravitational systems to new, better work elsewhere.

She made three successive career moves within about a five-year period in the tumultuous banking sector.

The turmoil of change became both the reason to leave and the reason that new, more desirable opportunities were being created elsewhere. After her first experience of receiving a severance package as part of a large downsizing, she realized:

- Severance is commonplace in this industry.
- You can tell when a downsizing is coming.
- You can try to position yourself to avoid being laid-off **OR**, you also can position yourself **to be laid off** and use the severance package as a way to fund a bit of savings and a productive, full-time work search.

As anyone knows who has tried to look for work while employed, it's really awkward. I've frequently had clients who are employed but trying to design a strategy to Move Out of a failing or struggling organization, and they frequently suffer from low search productivity because of the amount of time they are held prisoner by their jobs. I frequently offer the perverse-sounding observation, "The best thing that could happen to you is that you get laid off with a severance package so that you can dedicate uninterrupted attention to your search for better-fit work." It sounds like a dire piece of advice. **No one likes to unhook from income, but most rapidly realize that their best chance of finding or creating better work is truly limited while they are employed full-time.**

Tyler had also developed a good sense of timing about her departures. For her two subsequent layoff experiences, she saw it coming, volunteered for the layoff, and wound up with severance pay to put in the bank. There are times to wait to Move Out. But it's important to gauge whether or not severance will be offered and whether you can volunteer for the layoff. In an ironic situation, some have found that their work was quite valued by the organization, and they were not offered any options to participate (at least in the first round) in the layoff. Perhaps a retention bonus may come your way if your work is valued and the organization needs you to stay through the crucial downsizing. Trends in severance during the Great Recession have, not surprisingly, become less generous according to the report published by Lee Hecht Harrison, the global talent management firm. Gone are the bonanza days of hundreds of bank employees caught in a merger and being offered severance based on a length of service formula that generated six, seven, nine, and even twelve months of pay as part of their severance benefits. What severance benefits remain are more modest, but can be worth waiting for if it's a matter of staying another month in order to fund weeks or months of undistracted job search.

Clues of (mis)Fit with Your Job, Manager, Team, Organization

Only you can decide when it's time to Move Out of your current work. But let's look at some of the clues that suggest a misfit is building. We can use these clues to construct a picture of your current state of anxiety and concern about fit with your job, manager, team, organization. **There are four basic categories of evidence to consider:**

1. **Values/Beliefs**
2. **Emotions**
3. **Thoughts**
4. **Behaviors**

For any aspect of your work, virtually anything you observe, feel, or think about will fit in one of these four categories. If you're just starting to collect some specific clues, you can use these four categories to stimulate your thinking and observations as you scan your work environment for match-quality:

1. **Values**

Do your ethics or beliefs align? Knowledge, skills, and abilities may align while values do not. This isn't necessarily about "good versus evil" values conflicts. For example, maybe you firmly believe that your product offering will succeed only if it is controlled by the engineering function. But the new and predominant operational philosophy is that marketing and customer inputs will be the ruling force for product design and manufacturing. Can you live with that? Can you Adapt Your Style of operating and decision making to this new organizational value/belief?

2. **Emotions**

How do you feel about the job, boss, team, and organization? There may be negative feelings in too many of your weekly work encounters. You've outgrown the work, position, or team around you. No one has done anything wrong or bad; it's just that you're keenly aware of the loss of happiness, energy, and curiosity when you go to work each day. Can you manufacture internal passion for something? Probably not. It's not called passion if it's contrived.

3. **Thoughts (Cognitive)**

Are you learning? (See "When is it Time to Move Up?"). If no one cares about best practices or research and innovations, and knowledge is not collected nor used well, you may find yourself dissatisfied. Recall that the Chapter on "Moving Up" defined UP as more than just getting a promotion to a new level in a hierarchy. It's about moving to a new level of your own functioning and consciousness as a talent. If you're not learning, and the learning opportunities are diminishing rather than growing, start packing.

4. **Behaviors**

If the work is too dangerous, repetitive, strenuous, or psychologically stressful, you will experience a misfit. The style of interaction with colleagues or customers may be too confrontational, or perhaps management is absent or doesn't walk their talk.

"Dangerous or too strenuous" can start to matter at different times along your developmental timeline. Just had your first child? Just came home from double knee surgery? Just experienced the difficult death of a partner or family member with a chronic disease? Your definition of how your mind and body can cope is probably undergoing a change. Maybe your current work is unlikely to change in beneficial ways that match your immediate needs. Be sure to differentiate immediate or short-term needs from chronic or long-term needs.

The behaviors required by a new manager or a new company owner can be troubling. Suddenly having to work under very restrictive work rules due to a new union contract could be another example of daily behavioral requirements that may be too much of a stretch for you.

These four aspects are what you're dealing with as a set of thoughts and feelings about work and whether to stay or go. It is all these pieces of awareness that form the mental Tornado and keep circling in your thinking while wasting lots of your time. On the following page is a depiction of a simple way to start collecting these observations or impressions and building a picture of your current reality.

Write Now Exercise
MisFit Clues

For those of you who are a bit impatient and hate detail but are provoked by these categories of clues to collect, just write single, trigger words that remind you of your clues. Jot a few right in the box below. Yeah, *Write Now*. I started it for you...but ignore that, unless it fits.

Collecting Clues About (Mis)Fit with Your Current Work

	COGNITIVE What do I think/know about this? Am I getting smarter here?	EMOTIONAL What are the emotions and physical feelings I'm having?	VALUES What's at stake? What matters to me at each level at this time?	BEHAVIORAL How am I or other people acting, and do I like these behaviors?
AT THE LEVEL OF MY				
JOB				I'm on-time and ready while others just loiter
MANAGER	Smart		Harmony	
TEAM	Mental slackers		Doing the minimum	
ORGANIZATION		Low key		

It's important to have a method for systematically examining and evaluating your current work fit. The most repetitive or obvious annoyance can unduly influence your sense of fit, so it's important to aim for an objective and broader look. The subsequent assessment tool is designed to round out your sense of fit from many angles of view.

Questioning Your (mis)Fit at
Different Levels of Your Work

Now that you have had an initial opportunity to collect your overall sense of fit at the level of job, manager, team, and organization, let's dig a little deeper with some questions that will take your thinking, perhaps, to some new areas of consideration. While not a definitive list of criteria for fit, you'll explore next some of the dimensions to consider when trying to figure out why things may not seem right at this time. On the other hand, these same dimensions can be used to make a positive match or choice when you're prospecting and interviewing for your next work. These dimensions range from the micro to the macro levels.

Use your own body as a reminder of three dimensions of your work to check. We'll look at:

- **Head (cognitive)**: What do you need to know to be comfortable here? Are you spending your day thinking about problems, issues, needs, and trends that are engaging for you? Are you learning?
- **Heart (emotional and values)**: How do you feel when you're at work, and how are values espoused and lived where you work?
- **Hands (behavior, actions)**: What do you and others physically do, and how do you act at work? What observable behaviors and actions do you engage in and prefer or dislike?

Three-Level Assessment of Fit With Your Work

Instructions: Put a + or - next to each question based on whether that aspect of your work situation is currently positive or a GOOD FIT (+) for you in this area, or uncomfortable and a POOR FIT (-). Not sure? Not a good or bad fit? Not relevant to your work situation? In those cases, put a 0 in both.

+	-	QUESTIONS OF FIT
		With Your: JOB
		HEAD
		Do I know what it takes to accomplish my work at a quality level?
		Do I have enough education to comprehend the complexities of the job?
		Do I have the cognitive speed to process information, thoughts, and analyses with others?
		Do my problem solving and analysis methods get the results needed in the time allotted?
		HEART
		Do I want to come to work most days and do this work?
		Do I feel engaged with the work in a way that causes me to "go the extra mile" in a pinch?
		Do I share most of the values of the people I work with?
		Do I share most of the values of my customers or clients?
		Do I think this product or service is important?
		HANDS (Behavior)
		Is my physical workspace comfortable and safe, and does it enable my best work?
		Do I use physical capacities that are comfortable for me?
		Do I get to interact with people in a way and with a frequency that I like?
		Do I handle people or materials in ways that are comfortable for me?
		Am I expected to behave in a way that makes me embarrassed or angry? (Uncomfortable may be okay, since that's how we all feel if we haven't yet mastered a behavior. Embarrassed or angry? Not good.)
		With Your: MANAGER
		HEAD
		Does my boss understand my intellectual strengths (and weaknesses)?
		Do I respect my boss's intelligence and knowledge
		Does my knowledge base work with that of my boss?
		Is my education (amount or level) threatening to my boss?

		Can I articulate and think at a level that functions well with my boss?
		Does my boss have a helpful network and willingness to let me tap into it?
		HEART
		Do I like being around my boss as a person?
		Does my boss like being with me as a person?
		Do my boss and I share some significant values and interests?
		Does my boss have enough emotional intelligence and perceive it in others?
		Do my boss and I handle emotions in the workplace in a productive way? With each other? With others?
		Do I trust my boss to do the right/ethical thing?
		HANDS (Behavior)
		Does my energy level and speed match my boss—including his/her expectations in these two areas?
		Does my manager model the key competencies of the organization's leadership model?
		Does my manager model the organization's espoused values?
		Does she/he walk his own talk?
		Can I get help completing work from my boss?
		Does my boss micromanage and hover over my work?
		Do my physical work abilities duplicate or complement my boss's?
		Can my manager demonstrate skills or behaviors that are crucial for success?
		Can I get the level of training, coaching, or mentoring I need from this manager?
		Do either I or my boss experience physical intimidation from the other (intentional or unintentional)?
		Does my boss openly give constructive feedback and handle performance issues astutely?
		Does my boss show up in the workplace and make himself/herself available for discussions and questions?
		Does my boss create activities that build relationships beyond just doing work together?
		With Your: TEAM
		(You could be a member or manager of this team.)
		HEAD
		Is this a smart team, or do they over-rely on my knowledge?
		Is there the right balance of education and work-relevant knowledge on the team? (They're not always the same or even related.)
		Do I respect the knowledge in this team?

		Can the team members collaborate and share knowledge and information with me and each other?
		Can the team members learn together?
		HEART
		Do I like being with these team members?
		Do I feel accepted by the team?
		Do I accept all members of this team?
		Do we share enough values to cooperate and collaborate productively?
		Do I trust this team to do the right/ethical thing?
		Have I inspired followership if this is my team?
		Am I proud to mention that I'm a member of this team?
		Do we share the same model of leadership?
		Do we share the same model of decision-making and responsibility?
		HANDS (Behavior)
		Does this team work at the same energy level and pace that I do?
		Are all the right capabilities present to get the work done?
		Am I doing a fair and equitable amount of the team's production?
		Does the team look out for each other and pitch in to help someone who's struggling?
		Do people openly give constructive feedback?
		Does the team do things together to build relationships other than just work together?
		With Your: ORGANIZATION
		HEAD
		Is this is a learning organization? Is it getting smarter, and am I getting smarter?
		Is knowledge systematically transferred when someone senior is leaving?
		Is there adequate expertise to successfully accomplish the mission?
		Is there adequate competitive knowledge to be better than the rest?
		Do I aspire to acquire new knowledge at the rate the organization will require of me?
		Is the organization at a level of maturity that I like and in which I can thrive (start-up, ramp-up, stability, diversifying, expanding, contracting)?
		HEART
		Is the workforce engaged with the work of achieving the key goals?
		Is there a vision for the future that I am attracted to and want to participate in?
		Is there a mission that most people believe in?
		Is there a mission that I believe in?

		Is a management model, that I like, practiced here?
		Is there a set of organizational values that are practiced as espoused?
		Do I feel proud to say I work here?
		Is the organization concerned about the community in which it does business?
		Am I comfortable with the function that dominates the organization (engineering, finance, IT, etc.)?
		Are resources distributed throughout the organization in a way that I can support?
		Are there rewards and incentives for things I believe in?
		Does this place feel successful?
		HANDS (Behavior)
		Do leaders walk their talk (congruent with values, behaviors, and strategies espoused)?
		Does the leadership team work well with one another?
		Do leaders create relationships through activities other than just production work?
		Is the size of the organization comfortable for me to navigate, influence, and work in?
		Does the environment feel safe?
		Do people work with the right balance of team and individual effort?
		Is the work environment one that supports my productivity?
		Are the necessary productivity tools available to me to meet expectations and be successful?
		Are there systems and methods established that allow for productive efficiency?
		Does the organization have a planning style that fits me (structured, improv, nothing)?
		Are decisions made in a way that is comfortable for me?
		TOTALS

But Is It Significant?

Now comes the hard part: deciding if the balance of negatives to positives is troubling enough to cause you to want to Move Out. This is where it's crucial to have a Think Out Loud Laboratory where you can discuss your observations with someone whose judgment you trust. You need to hear yourself talk about these observations regarding fit, and you need to hear yourself respond to the questions that a good listener will ask to get clarification.

Fast-Forward Fantasy

Before heading over to the Think Out Loud Lab, there is one test you can run to see if your overall assessment of fit is suggesting a "stay" or "go" strategy. We want to harvest some of your intuition and subconscious impressions of your current work, and see what they suggest.

One of the ways to open up your perspective on any decision or choice that you struggle with is to get out of the present and extend your time-frame to include the future. We often get stuck in hyper-analysis of facts and options that are grounded in memories of the recent past and the possibilities of the present. These possibilities are not irrelevant, but they may not be sufficient to produce the insights and breakthrough thinking needed to decide on your next move. This is a time to widen the frame on your mental movie about your situation and options, and include fast-forward elements.

Failing the Fast-Forward Fantasy

"Should I stay with this firm or not?" This question had been cycling and recycling in Randy's thinking for the last three months, and he was moving no closer to an answer. He had been carefully observing and compiling a list of all the positive and negative aspects of working in a founder-run advertising firm, with twenty-five employees, located in a mid-sized city on the East Coast. Each time he went through his pro-con list, he wound up with a tie score and a feeling of ambivalence about staying or leaving. In the meantime, he remained frustrated in his daily work by inadequate IT resources and the increase in situations in which he was told to just "make it work" with new client assignments that were grossly mismatched to the firm's capabilities.

His career consultant made a practical suggestion to break the endless tie-score in this mental tug of war: "Expand your time-frame of consideration to include the future that you can reasonably imagine to exist here in the next eighteen to twenty-four months. Instead of treading water in your job—while being increasingly disengaged from the work and waiting for more data or impressions to come in—let's project the future and see if it's worth staying around for."

Randy had been with the firm for three years and had a very reasonable ability to infer what might happen in the near future. As he projected fast-forward, a picture of what awaited him became clear, and he realized the following four truths:

1. The founder-owner wasn't going anywhere and was unmotivated to change her micro-managing leadership style.
2. The firm's three middle management positions were unlikely to open up in the next two years.
3. Even if he were promoted to one of the middle manager roles, he wouldn't enjoy working with the other two peer managers.
4. If he got a promotion, the middle manager role would have little real development associated with it because the founder-owner's style really didn't allow for growth or autonomy so much as just more opportunity to follow her direction on practically everything.

The firm turned out to be a place that failed the *fast-forward fantasy*. Even if these current issues (IT resources and better prospect matching) were resolved, he would evolve forward into a future that he really didn't want to be part of. Even if Randy progressed at the firm, his future picture would likely still contain significant, structural flaws that would make the place a poor fit for his future professional work. Dilemma over. It was time to pull the rip-cord and plan an exit and search strategy.

Hopefully the Questions of Fit assessment caused you to be aware of some aspects of good fit that you might not have realized—perhaps due to an immediate problem that has dominated your focus of attention. This exercise certainly allowed you to be more specific about many aspects of work. If you're ambivalent about where the assessment leaves you, and your trip to the Think Out Loud Lab with a trusted, good listener didn't lead to an "ah ha" breakthrough moment about your current work, then it's time to get greedy, fantasize, and engage in some *criminal thinking*.

The Job You'd Like to Steal

Be curious, and start to do some casual research and field observations about the job you'd like to *steal*. I'm not talking about the job you think you can interview for or get promoted to. I'm not necessarily talking about the job you deserve or are qualified for. I'm talking about the work you've seen or read about someone else doing and been so attracted to that you think you'd love it—and if you don't really deserve it (yet) you might have to steal it to get access to it.

If something came to mind right as you were reading that paragraph, write it down in the margins of this page. Now!

Write Now Exercise
Thought Experiment

So let's just say you could get some intriguing job by *taking it* from the person who has it now; and, once you did, you'd suddenly be endowed with everything necessary to successfully do that job. How does it feel just to consider that?

- Start jotting down a brief list of the Head, Heart, and Hands aspects of the work that are so appealing to you—such as skills you love to use; people contact [or lack of it] that is attractive; money; fame; power; physical, intellectual or emotional aspects of the job; social impact; travel; etc.

#1 STOLEN JOB/WORK _____

Head:

Heart:

Hands:

#2 STOLEN JOB/WORK _____

Head:

Heart:

Hands:

- What would others say when they discovered you'd gotten this job? ("Cool. It's you." "What the hell are you thinking?" "Great, and it's about time." "Don't give up your day-job.")
- How long do you think you'd stay interested in this work?

Here is how you can use this information: Embedded in the things you've written down about the job you'd like to steal are the clues to the unmet needs you have today. Some may be fantasy and not likely to ever be fulfilled (such as being a billionaire movie actor), but even those fantasies provide clues to the "missing nutrients" in your current, average, daily serving of work.

As you identify the attractive aspects of the job you'd like to steal, start looking for them in the actual work that is around you—work of friends, colleagues, co-workers, famous people, or others. We're looking for living examples of work that could embody more elements you crave, keeping in mind that they don't necessarily have to come in the form of paid work. Play, hobbies, volunteering, and goofing off all could give you access to non-paid aspects of what you crave.

Case Study
The Urge to Perform

Beth had developed quite a career as a software engineer, working now for a major test and measurement company with their embedded software. As an energetic woman with beautiful, flaming, red hair and an active, ironic sense of humor, let's just say she sort of stood out in a field of deadly serious, shy, and introverted software geeks.

When Beth did the Questions of Fit assessment, she found a slightly out-of-balance scorecard with slightly more things that were not fitting than fitting. Nothing was significantly troubling, but there was still a sense that something was missing.

The thought experiment appealed to the kid in her and her sense of play. When she identified *talk-show host* as her job-to-steal, she astutely noticed that neither Jimmy Fallon nor Letterman were looking at the exit door; and so, she started to look a little more closely at her daily surroundings of people who were using some of the same behaviors and skills as a talk-show host.

She recalled that the trainer/facilitator who ran the last leadership training class she attended was engaged in a surprising amount of the same activities as her fantasy job: interviewing people in the class and asking good questions, facilitating discussion without having all the answers, being in charge of the "show," conducting exercises, and—most exciting of all—getting to use humor throughout the day as part of the facilitation process.

Beth approached the manager of training and development with the idea of a rotation in his department. *Sold.* In fact, *win-win.* When training engineers who are struggling to learn management skills, instant credibility is built when the training facilitator happens also to have an engineering degree.

Best of all, Beth could facilitate a fun learning environment using her ironic sense of humor. BONUS: As an engineer, there were no engineer jokes that she was disqualified from telling.

Eagerly Attempting to Answer the Wrong Question

There is an important lesson in the story about Beth and her desire to engage, entertain, and introduce humor at work. When she first spoke of her career ambivalence, she was pretty convinced that she was on the verge of pulling the rip-cord and leaving her job and employer to overcome her sense of dread about going to work every day.

More than 25 percent of all my clients during my fifteen years of career consulting have come to me with a white-knuckle grip on their career rip-cord, eagerly attempting to answer the wrong question. Most were way too eager, as was Beth, to focus on Move Out? as their primary question. In being so over-eager and anxious, they had totally overlooked better opportunities that were much closer at hand and easier to attain.

This is why The Three Career Questions are built to work together as a guidance system or model. They aren't three separate and independent questions. They need to be addressed as a set to make sure you're getting the check and balance quality they can offer as a system. In the next table are examples of some "wrong questions" that clients have come to me to reinterpret. They had an uneasy sense that they weren't pursuing the right question, and came to the Think Out Loud Lab to search for a more appropriate question to pursue.

Wrong Question	Why It Seemed Right	Right Question	Why It Was the Better Question
Is it time to Move Up in this firm?	*I'm bright. I'm bored.*	Is it time to Adapt My Style?	*I was smart but not a leader. I managed my boss well but didn't inspire followers.*
Is it time to Adapt My Style?	*I'm not developing followership and a team spirit with the production floor team.*	Is it time to Move Up? *I want to be on the corporate marketing team.*	*In the frantic start-up of the company, I was put in charge of production; but my innate talent is in the graphic and visual world of marketing, not in the concrete world of manufacturing.*
Is it time to Move Out?	*My new boss doesn't get me. She's over-focused on my finance background, but I'm interested in doing more organizational development and change management.*	Is it time to Adapt My Style?	*My previous boss knew how to leverage my real skills and thus activate my passion, but he retired. Now, I need to be more of a self-marketing agent and promoter of my skills so I'm not dependent on others (my new boss) being perceptive enough to know my strengths and route me into the appropriate roles.*

If all of your collected clues seem to confirm that it really is time to Move Out, then pay attention to refining your targets of interest first, before you quit your current work and income source. You will eventually spend a lot of valuable time and energy applying to jobs or starting an entrepreneurial venture. It almost always takes more time than you might expect, so do your research while you have an income source to fund it. At some point, many work searches require time and flexibility that aren't possible if you're fully employed. **When and if you choose to quit, you'll want to have your personal marketing plan well focused and ready to implement quickly since you'll be living and working off of savings.**

Get your talents understood and focused on the work that you can do best and love most. Hundreds of comprehensive job search books will lay out those steps. An equal number of books will help you decide if you're entrepreneurial and can make a business idea a reality and run it successfully. But you should experience some considerable relief if you've begun to answer the question, "Is it time to Move Out?" and used the various tools in this chapter to confirm your sense that *yes, it's time.*

About to Be Invited to Leave

There are times when the clues about leaving are not just about your sense of fit with the work, but more about external factors that are changing and indicating that you may be in for an involuntary move-out. Let's prime your radar to spot some classic indicators of when it's time to get ready to leave because your boss may be about to invite you to do so.

Clues for "Invited to Leave"

Some classic pieces of evidence frequently show up in misfit or devolving work situations. Each of these fits in our criteria category of Behavioral/Activity. These are actions that may be done to you, or done throughout your organization, representing a more generalized threat to the jobs of many.

10 Negative Changes or Conditions to Watch For:

1. **You're Not Consulted.** Losing your chances for input in organizational matters is a signal that leaders are getting closer to running affairs without you.

2. **You're Being Scrutinized More Closely.** You feel as if you're not trusted. Micromanagement and documentation of your work has begun.

3. **Co-workers Are Not Conferring with You.** You're being left out of meetings you've usually been part of. It's been a while since anyone's discussed a future project with you.

4. **You Got a Poor Performance Rating.** You barely got a raise and perhaps even received a warning. You and your boss don't share the same perspectives as to why this happened or even that it happened.

5. **You've Had Frequent Run-ins With Your Boss.** While people claim it's not personal, job security often comes down to relationships. Performance is subjective, and managers are more likely to let go of people who make them feel uncomfortable. Eventually the clashes stop, and you'll find yourself ignored.

6. **There's a Lot of Talk About "Transition."** Your company is likely to merge, be acquired, or "reorganize," and your company leader is not prominent in the messaging about the future. Change can represent new opportunities if you have positioned yourself and not let others over-define you. Beware of the viability of your product, service, and impact at a time like this.

7. **New-Hires Are the Salvation of the Organization's Future.** New folks are being hired who can do no wrong with the higher-ups. Your development plateaued. A merger or acquisition brought new talent to the company, and they

seem to rule. Certain academic degrees or professional certifications (that you may not have) are suddenly very important.

8. **Your New Boss From the Opposite Coast Isn't House Hunting.** Your old boss was suddenly replaced by an executive on loan from another region or division of the company, which could easily absorb your function rather than accommodate your job.

9. **Training or Development Activities Are No Longer Encouraged Nor Funded.** Your performance reviews don't include a meaningful development plan or discussion, and there is only a vague sense of what the future looks like in terms of products, markets, or specific work for you.

10. **Leadership: Your Manager Is a Puzzle, Obstacle, or Entanglement.** The surveys keep showing the same fact: people more frequently quit their bosses, not the jobs or organizations. Their resignation doesn't have to be attributed to any terrible, evil, or overly negative traits in the boss. He or she is an expediter of your talent, and so you must make a judgment call about your chances of developing or being able to adapt to this person so as to work with him/her more comfortably.

Here are three ways that a relationship with a boss can derail without malice or ill intent on anyone's part. It may feel like a problem but try reframing it.

There is a great Chinese saying that suggests redefining a "problem" as a:

- **Puzzle**: You are unable to get a clear or consistent reading as to your boss's style and needs, and therefore unsure how to work with her. Other people aren't able to help solve the puzzle either. Everyone is working around or avoiding this leader.

- **Obstacle**: Your boss needs to be the smartest person involved with all work problems, issues, or needs. Your boss perceives you as a threat or distraction and needs to keep you assigned to less than critical work. Your boss perceives you as inadequate in your position or inadequate compared to himself and starts to side-line your development or assignment to crucial work.

- **Entanglement**: Your boss unnecessarily inserts herself into people's work and also has crucial political relationships within the company that she holds very close. Subsequently, you've become over-reliant on her ability to access these people, and since you're discouraged (by her) from interacting with them to develop your own relationships, you've become pretty entangled with your boss.

Do You Fit the Profession?

We have looked at your work fit in terms of how it plays out at various levels: job, boss, team, and organization. There is one other realm of fit that is crucial too: *profession*. Yes, it's possible to be in a profession and not necessarily be a good fit for it. The atmosphere in certain professions can change and cause your degree of fit to increase or decrease.

Think about the number of people who entered the teaching profession under the assumption that they'd be dealing with twenty to twenty-five students who were prepared to learn in an innovative classroom that the teacher designed and controlled. When these teachers graduated from college and got their teaching credentials, they found that the profession of teaching involved adjusting to classrooms they didn't control which were filled with up to thirty-five students. It also included being constricted by regulated, dictated teaching outcomes that caused teachers to "teach to the test" rather than to any innovative curriculum they might create.

Medical professionals are in the same state of shock. They may have entered the profession as well-paid, independent practitioners with specialties in adolescent psychiatry. But the profession and medical field transformed around them and left them in a profession and marketplace that is no longer a fit. They actually have a lower income than they did seven years ago. Their treatment modalities are driven by the insurance coverage of their patients, not their personal strengths as clinicians. They have found themselves forced to abandon their comfortable private practices to join medical groups for economies of scale—thus joining in with all the headaches that come with doing things in a group.

Being in a profession is no guarantee of a perpetually comfortable set of work circumstances. There are adaptations and even total exit plans that many people will execute after their initial participation in a given professional field. But the facts indicate that having a profession is more durable and vital than not having a profession or professional identity. There are many types of work that call themselves professions which are less well defined than, let's say, that of physicians, engineers, or rabbis. The criteria we will explore next are indicators of the vitality and durability of occupations—not of your job, boss, team, or organization, but the type of professional work you've chosen. Some areas of professional endeavor are more vital than others, and it's important to know how to assess the work you're doing for its level of vitality.

Career Vitality Criteria

Caela Farren, PhD, in her book, *Who's Running Your Career: Creating Stable Work in Unstable Times,* suggests eight criteria to help you gauge the viability of the professional work and identity that you've created for yourself. How many of the following eight criteria do you have supporting your current work?

Your Profession/Work Is Vital if It:

1. **Is essential to the purpose of the organization you work for.** Your professional work has more vitality if it would be difficult (not impossible) to outsource. This has changed over time. Look at how many manufacturing and even human resources functions are provided from outside organizations that used to consider these same functions part of the essential fabric of an organization.

2. **Your skill and work transfers to other industries and organizations.** A professional identity as an "Industrial Production Layout Manager" can help you be seen as having transferable and useful skills for setting up a variable production floor in a commercial bakery or a metal fabrication shop: two very different industries. A professional identity as a "Hummer Frame Layout Manager" over-identifies you with a limited product and company attachment. Your job title might as well read "Dinosaur Wrangler." **Remember,** you are not your job title.

If you are considering Moving Out to another line of work or job, here is an exercise that will help you document how your work can transfer to other organizations or industries. It is important to collect information about your credibility and transferability to other industries as you meet people or encounter information and intuitions about other forms of work. Don't try to hold all these insights or encounters in your head. Start recording them here.

How Can I Transfer My Talent?

If you are in the process of Moving Out of a job or even a profession, the following exercise will help you focus on making a move to another likely industry or organization where your skills are transferable and your credibility is likely to be high.

Key Term

"Crediblility" means you have become known and can be <u>preferred</u> over other candidates because you are perceived as:

- Knowing key players;
- Having accurate perceptions;
- Producing results;
- Acting with speed and having relevant skills;
- Knowing the market context:
    - Strengths
    - Weaknesses
    - Opportunities
    - Threats

Write Now Exercise

In this exercise, you will be asked to expand your job search, list target organizations outside your current industry, and list job titles you could hold as well as results you could produce in these jobs.

To start building your list of people and organizations that are targets of interest (because they are logically related to prospective work that you could do), make notes next to the prompts below as you look both upstream and downstream from your current location into the value stream of your work.

Upstream:
- Name of suppliers, vendors, consultants, channel partners, organizations, consulting firms, or referral agents

- Job titles or roles of interest to you

- Business results or output you could produce in or for these organizations

Current Industry/Market:
- Name of *competitor* organizations

- Name of job titles or roles that interest you

- Business results or output you could produce in these organizations

Exercise continues, keep reading

Downstream:

- Name of *customers, distributors, regulators, monitors or analyst* organizations

- Name of job titles or roles of interest to you

- Business results or output you could produce in these organizations

3. **Include competencies that apply to other professions.** An investigative journalist has key competencies such as: research, structured interviewing, question construction, report writing, using networks to find information, summarizing complexity, and managing details. As newspaper publishers were dropping like flies and searching for a way to support their reporting and editorial staffs, an astute journalist client of mine who was designing his exit strategy from the newspaper industry noticed something important about his profession's viability: his competencies were very similar to those of "investigators" working in the judicial system and for insurance companies. That viability and professional vitality fueled his Move Out of the

newspaper business (which was in bankruptcy) and into an insurance company of sufficient size that eventually he could Move Up into his ultimate target work of corporate communications.

4. **Provides *personal* and financial compensation.** Personal compensation refers to the rewards that are outside of just the salary and bonus checks. Factors such as location, flexibility, organizational reputation and values, camaraderie, learning opportunities, office environment, safety, and other rewards may make your current profession viable and vital for you and for many other colleagues. Work that is pursued for income potential alone tends to be less viable— and lives and dies by the employer's rule of, "What have you done for me today?"

5. **Has professional associations that represent it (even if you don't bother to become a member).** These associations represent a form of marketplace recognition, legitimacy, and a source of both development and quality control of professional members. And guess what? They make a better impact on your career if you join them, not just point at them from the outside or list them on your resume because you once went to a meeting (which is bogus).

6. **Has an obvious path to mastery.** Here's a great source of guidance that is also related to our first question: when is it time to Move Up? Professional associations (such as the Institute of Management Consultants), or even some large corporations (like Intel) or professional service firms (such as a large law firm), will identify core competencies, degrees of proficiency, and experience required for their core professions (consultants, engineers, and lawyers). Not only can you track your progress within the profession, but others can sense your level of mastery by referencing the professional framework provided.

7. **Is age-independent.** Compare the limiting quality of the age factor in professions of Circus Marketing Director versus Acrobat in the Circus. Enough said. A profession with great vitality doesn't emphasize age as a crucial criteria for success.

8. **Requires communication outside the organization.** Not just a little communication either. For example, human resources professionals can become quite inwardly focused in their attempts to service their employee populations. A machinist can work a machine with great skill, keep her head down, make quota every week, and have no idea where to look for work when the company closes down. The lack of outward focus leads to a limited network—creating a dangerous limit on mobility. But, did you ever notice how much faster and easier sales professionals seem to land their next jobs? Not by coincidence, their work takes place every day in a living network, and they benefit from it when it's time to Move Out.

Well, how did you do? Now is the time to analyze how much of your current circumstances you can change or influence to get a higher degree of career vitality and fit with your job, team, boss, and organization. If there is little opportunity for change or influence, then it's time for a well-designed and executed exit strategy.

Time to Exit

So, you've read the criteria for match-qualities. You've done the gut test, and your stomach is overdue for some relief from this emotional churn about your work. This is a book about asking the right questions to know *when* to exit not how to conduct a job search. There are only about 50,000 books about that topic, and the point here is not to make it 50,001.

All exits can't be perfect. Leaving some jobs or employers will feel just plain painful, aggravating, conflicted, and sad. Other exits will be experienced with an enormous sense of relief and an actual bodily sense of lightness. But, too often exits or endings are experienced with an un-ceremonial sense of ambivalence. We're just *not sure*. This is where we need a plan and the capacity to develop a sense of decisiveness about the exit and what's next.

Sarah Lawrence-Lightfoot said, while discussing her book, *Exits: The Ending That Set Us Free* (Sarah Critchton Books, 2012), "In our own individual development, the trajectory of our life stories [has] within them these entrances and exits, you know, that at each time when we are moving into a next stage in our lives, there is this tug of war between moving forward and staying put, between progression and regression."

Psychologist, Eric Erikson, talked about this fifty years ago, "And to move forward to the next level, we need to exit. So exit is a moment of great propulsion." (NPR, "Talk of the Nation" interview, June 11, 2012).

So, how can we experience our exits from jobs or bodies of work as involving propulsion toward the next engagements or, at least, our next sources of satisfaction? Recall our discussion of orbital mechanics in Chapter 2. The point of orbital mechanics is to enable a spacecraft to get added propulsion energy from a planet that it flies close to. If we have a career strategy and are flying toward the right work and organizations, we should be gaining momentum or propulsion energy that finds us exiting or leaving current work with increased experience, skill and the power to move forward. That's what we now want to harvest so as to limit the time we spend in ambivalence or spinning our thoughts in our mental Tornado.

Outward Focus

Prior to Moving Out of an organization or a role, there will be a series of insights and refinements about your understanding of the following three areas:

1. Yourself and your knowledge, interests, skills, style, and abilities
2. Your updated understanding of your values and the kind of work that satisfies you
3. Your knowledge of the places in the market that may have that kind of work

It is the third insight that we want to strengthen with an outside focus as you hunt down the available work in various organizations that are a fit for you. I want to offer you a questioning tool so that you can better focus your attention outward on market research and networking. It's called a *Focus of Inquiry* (FOI) and, what a surprise, it uses questions as a way to maintain awareness of your market and where your skills and experience can best contribute next.

Your Focus of Inquiry contains key questions that act as scanning radar for your probe into career space. Just like a real space probe journeying through our solar system, you need to know where you are relative to your target and other important objects and forces along your path. By asking astute questions, you can harness the embedded intelligence of other people in the marketplace and keep yourself well positioned to link your strengths with the needs of the market.

Key Term

Your **Focus of Inquiry** will guide your inquiry into the four elements that drive the creation of work: problems, issues, needs, and trends.

When it's time to exit a current job and organization, people often realize how long they have had their heads down and focused on their jobs and organizations and, therefore, how much they've lost touch with what's going on out in the expansive and dynamic space called the market.

You can't afford to be off course and forget to check your radar for too long these days. The nature and pace of changes in many markets requires accurate monitoring. Making frequent micro adjustments to stay your course is a lot easier than realizing you've overshot a market turn and have to spend valuable fuel and time to get back on course with costly changes to your education, credentialing, certifications, geography, or salary.

So in a best case scenario, you've been alert and monitoring your career radar screen. You've kept an informed eye on the marketplace of ideas and opportunities, and you are either:

- On a career course that is satisfying and worth maintaining (just with a different employer).
- Ready to change career course and start researching and probing with questions that will help you find work that is a better fit with who you are becoming.

Start By Asking *Who?* The Power of Your Network

Unfortunately, many people construct their exit strategies around *where*. They spend too much time too early in the process trying to identify the jobs or organizations in which they want to land even when they're not yet clear on the work they really want to do. *They just want a job.*

Key Term

Quickly review the definition of career management. **Career Management** is the art of managing one's relationship to work over a lifetime by maximizing insights that are intrapersonal, interpersonal, and market-based—and turning them into action strategies.

While it will be essential to eventually clarify where you want to work, I would like to suggest you start your search by obtaining practical, contemporary information about the work you really want to do. The most compelling and relevant information of this nature is obtained through real people working in the real marketplace. **Start by asking *Who?*** Who are the key people in your network of friends, relatives, neighbors, friends-of-friends, colleagues, softball teammates, etc. who can make you smarter about the work in your target market that needs your talent to get it done? Who can help you identify the marketplace problems, issues, needs, and trends that are of personal and professional interest to you? Work lurks behind problems, issues, needs, and trends. You must connect to these four elements by demonstrating or suggesting your ability to provide solutions, insights, resources, and positioning ideas as a product of your talents and ability to accomplish real work—not just your desire to have a job.

Much of the information and insight we need is found through asking questions and extracting information from the imbedded intelligence of the marketplace—the marketplace of ideas and the people WHO surround you. It's time to develop a genuine curiosity about the knowledge others carry in their heads—as well as their stories explaining how they came to their knowledge, opinions, and abilities.

The marketplace of ideas is the place you go to trade non-material value including ideas, innovations, information, and perspectives.

In this process, we want to answer the following two questions:
1. What do people know or believe to be true about the marketplace around us?
2. What are their perceived organizational needs for talent to be applied to:
   - Problems
   - Issues

- Needs
- Trends?

In the marketplace of ideas, we can solicit stories and descriptions that also include peoples' needs and desires. We discover the talents, experiences, and answers that they are currently searching for along with the work they need to have accomplished. ***This is the real treasure to be discovered: the work that needs to be done.***

The marketplace of ideas contains information about unmet needs, unanswered questions, unsolved problems, and untapped trends. Career Self-Reliance and the management of your career cycle requires being more aware of the work that our communities (commercial, social, and spiritual) need to have performed—not just the jobs waiting to be filled. Work does not always come neatly packaged as a job.

Case Study
The Untapped Gold Mine

Mike was winding up his long and successful partnership in a prestigious law firm as they wound down his real estate practice specialty within the firm. The dilemma facing him was less about what his next source of income might be (but that was real too) and more about how to face the marketplace full of ideas that interested him more than practicing law.

His background was a treasure trove (or was it a Tornado?) of education and areas of civic engagement that stretched far beyond the practice of law. It included degrees in engineering, anthropology, public administration, and law—as well as leadership in political, commercial, spiritual, and law communities. Most of all, he was a skilled and diplomatic communicator. It was time to take full advantage of those qualities when doing his market research.

After admitting that his area of law was on the decline, both throughout the marketplace and in his own head and heart, the plan was to engage in massive dialogue with his substantial network. The job market was easy to explore quickly. There was practically nothing for a senior professional like Mike. But both the marketplace and the civic arena were filled with problems, issues, needs, and trends that could utilize someone like him.

His dialogue with the marketplace was constructed around two of his *motivated competencies* (skills and abilities that you have a strong motivation to use in your work). Mike identified two important things in our career assessment and in his past work history:

1. His tendency to be a "bridge brain." He held a strong capacity to construct a mental and emotional bridge between differing points of view—thus building comprehensive empathy and understanding with others.

2. His strong value on, and capacity to create, centrist positions that made sense to others in a dialogue. His dialogue with others in his network produced vigorous head-nodding agreements about the perils and frustrations of political and ideological silos that were slowing progress on any number of political fronts. And a second phenomenon emerged: people seldom pointed him to jobs that were open, although it did happen a couple of times. Instead, his network kept pointing him to the same thought leaders in the same consulting firm. It became his lost tribe. Everyone kept mentioning things such as, "Hey, have you talked to the people over at XYZ Consulting? They do interesting stuff in this area."

With multiple overlapping introductions, his eventual meeting with the principles of the firm was practically like a reunion. Their dialogue was filled with references to colleagues they had in common, affirmative nods about approaches to key issues, and the tendency to finish each other's sentences. This convergence of like-minded professionals was no coincidence. Mike's entire network of colleagues pointed him to XYZ because they were responding to the ample clues he offered as to his best and highest purpose, and which marketplace needs he was most compelled to address. The two founding partners at XYZ were interested, because they were looking to replace themselves in the coming years. They were thrilled to find a senior, well-connected business and political professional like Mike who could enhance their team.

Dialogue, backed by a focusing strategy, made the difference when Mike engaged his network. His network had an embedded intelligence that he tapped in this process. The results were beyond positive. But, more importantly, similar results are completely reproducible by anyone who can construct an astute dialogue within his or her network.

You may have heard the term, "hidden job market." No, it's not an evil plot or a sinister secret. **At any given time in our economy, the majority of work opportunities are not publicly advertised or published in print or electronic media.** Most of the work needing to be done in the marketplace (anything from marketing campaigns and sales to financial planning, engineering, or aerobics instruction) is waiting to be matched to the right talent. When the talent appears, the employer then will turn the *work they need accomplished* into *a job* or contract of some kind—not the other way around.

This reality requires us to have a form of career management and marketplace savvy that looks beyond the published sources of job listings, though these traditional sources can't be ignored. What we need is a *Focus of Inquiry:* a smart way to aim our attention into the market and find the work that needs to be done. To do that, as mentioned, we first harness the imbedded intelligence of our personal network. Subsequently, we tap into the wider marketplace of ideas to which our network can introduce us. The focused inquiry starts with the People Who Know and Love You—your inner circle—and expands to include the *relevant introductions they'll make to people in the marketplace who have work that needs to be done.*

Our Focus of Inquiry will be our agenda, our starting point, to launch conversations and know what we're going to talk about when we start to network. This is the tool, as you'll read about next, that answers the question, "What should I talk about or ask when I network with my key contacts?" It will literally act as your call plan or agenda as you talk with and meet face-to-face with your networking partners.

In addition to your personal network and those who they know, there are professional and community associations that are sources of like-minded colleagues or fellow tribe members—seeing and valuing things in ways that might be similar to you. Shortly after you establish yourself in a functional area of expertise, you need to join professional associations that represent the interests and professional standards of your specialty. We'll explore more in depth about this in Chapter 7: *Leveraging Professional Associations in Your Career Management Strategy.*

As we've explored in this book, your professional tribe will stand you in good stead when it's time to Move Up, Move Out of your current organization, or learn ways to Adapt Your Style for greater success where you currently work. There are associations for independent consultants (for example, the Institute of Management Consultants), social service agency directors (such as United Way), and various mechanical professions (like the American Electronics Association) that will enable you to start your market research or confirm research you've already done with live conversations and real-time information.

According to the Center for Association Leadership, in 2009 there were 90,908 trade and professional associations in the United States. Each association is a lightning rod that conducts all the hot issues for that profession or trade group and interprets what they mean for their members and the rest of society. That type of concentrated information, perspective, and involvement makes such organizations and their meetings, conferences, and training events a crucial area of activity for good networking-driven research into preferred areas of work.

But one caution about association events: don't just attend the events for your profession. You're not all that unique when you have a finance degree in a room full of other finance professionals at a Financial Executives International meeting. In fact, other finance professionals who are looking for work are likely to be attending such a meeting and competing for the same work. So, why not also attend meetings where you're a bit unique and less likely to be researching work with people who are your most likely competitors?

If you are a financial professional in Texas or Oklahoma and exploring the oil industry, you might want to consider attending a meeting of the American Society of Petroleum Geologists. It will be nice to be treated as a visiting professional, and you might even learn a few things. You're unique in that setting; people will give you a different type of attention than if you were in a room filled with other CPAs just like you.

The Work of Networking and the Question That Has Plagued WoMan Throughout History: "What Exactly Do I Talk About if I'm Not Asking for a Job?"

So much (maybe too much) has been written about networking methods and techniques and the importance of doing it in a way that doesn't find you simply asking everyone if they know of any job openings. This chapter is not a rehash of that body of existing knowledge about networking. Let's just assume you understand the importance of networking, whether you enjoy it or not is another question. And again, rule number one: networking is not asking for a job. It's an interpersonal exchange of information between two people who share a common interest which may be a mutual friend or colleague as well as subject matter. This shared interest precedes the process of finding out where there is work that needs to be done, or a job.

Here's an unfortunate truism about our contemporary work culture: people generally don't want to spend their time finding *you* work or managing *your* career unless they are:

- Your spouse (this source of help wears thin fast)
- Your mother (this source of help has already worn thin)
- Your questionable boyfriend/girlfriend (who is eager for you to afford your own place)
- A best friend to whom you owe a lot of money (who may have slightly compromised objectivity, wouldn't you say?)
- Your parole officer (you may have some career management issues this book won't address)
- A career management consultant or career coach

"But wait," I hear you say. "Don't *recruiters* want to help me find a job?" Well, they certainly like the end result of filling a job opening (when they get paid), but you need to be very clear about who their customer is and, hence, their primary motivation, focus, and payoff. They are busy fulfilling the needs of the organization that pays them, not a job hunter or career changer. Recruiters want to match a talent to a defined need inside an organization. Then they want to move right on to doing it again with another client company, and then again and again. Unless you're an ideal match for the position they need to fill, they are not able to spend their time discussing and helping to shape your career strategy.

So where's the love? If most people aren't waiting to jump on your career management bandwagon and work on your campaign, how does networking figure into a career management strategy so heavily? Answer: *information* and *insight*. These two invaluable factors are imbedded in the ambient IQ of the marketplace of ideas. Networking un-embeds information and insight, and leads you to real work that needs to be done.

Don't Think of This As "Networking"...
It's "Network-Driven Research"

Network-driven research is the *exchange* of information between two people who have a *shared* interest and, ideally, share a colleague in common who introduces them. Your network will need to make introductions so that you will be working from a *warm* referral. There should be minimal cold calls to people you don't know at all.

Pay attention to the key words in the definition above: "*exchange*" and "*shared*." Good networkers bring information and ideas to the conversation. They are not there merely to take information, that's what a novice or amateur does. Also, they consistently link to people on the basis of some common interest. The common point of reference may be an idea, an experience, or a person who they both know. But, cold calls are just that, cold, and they seldom (not never) lead to productive, substantial conversations or relationships unless you're incredibly attractive and sitting in a singles bar.

The exchange of information during networking is based on an agenda, or Focus of Inquiry (FOI), that simply uses thoughtful questions to guide your inquiry into problems, issues, needs, and trends that matter to you and the other person. The actual conversations can range from very formal inquiries with a straight-laced subject matter expert (such as a high-level/high-tech executive, commodities trader, or circuit court judge), who has a very tight time schedule and little time to chat or explore—to something that is more like a conversational dance with an intellectual partner who is open to "going steady" because you're asking engaging questions like a professional peer would.

Your *Focus of Inquiry*

Your questions and conversations need to start by being about something other than j-o-b-s.

Key Term

Your **Focus of Inquiry** (FOI) is your plan for conducting market research into work that needs to be done.

By getting the people in your network to talk about *problems, issues, needs, and trends* that are of interest to you and relevant to them, you create the chance to discover and offer *solutions, innovations, resources, and positioning ideas* that you can provide. At that point, your questions and the conversation have begun to uncover clues about work that needs to be done—perhaps by you.

Let's break down this FOI into parts. We'll see how you can create one for your own network-driven research.

The Focus of Inquiry Starts with Two Key Parts:

1. A role you assign to yourself and a frame of mind to be in as you network
2. A PINT (problems, issues, needs, and trends) analysis

1. **Your Role = S.I.P.** The role I suggest you give yourself is that of *Successful Inquiring Professional* (SIP). Try that on for size. Does that feel better than being a "networker" or an "informational interviewer"? The point is not to put this on your business card or leave voicemail messages with that as your title. The value of thinking about this role definition is that it keeps you in a certain frame of mind so that you both act and respond in compelling ways. You wouldn't put "Job Seeker" or "Career Changer" on your business card either, but think of the different image and atmosphere you would create in a dialogue wherein you portrayed yourself as a "job seeker" versus a "successful inquiring professional."

2. **Now that you're a SIP, you need a PINT.** Haven't you always wanted someone to tell you that you needed a PINT to do better networking?

Actually you need a PINT Analysis. There are four topics you need to study in the markets that you are targeting for work. They comprise the PINT Analysis:

1. **P**roblems
2. **I**ssues (Nothing broken or wrong—for example, new regulations, pending legislation, new CEO)
3. **N**eeds
4. **T**rends

We know that *work lurks* behind each of these four topics. Getting smart about these four topics allows you insights into the work that needs to be done in the market you're targeting. As you discuss them, you'll pick up information and an understanding valuable to you and valuable enough to pass on to others with whom you network during your inquiry. They will be interested in:

- Solutions to **Problems;**
- Innovations to address **Issues;**
- Resources to fill **Needs;**
- Positioning ideas to exploit **Trends.**

Here's how to visualize the fact that work is at the center of our inquiry.

Focus of Inquiry Leads You to Work That Needs to Be Done (by You)

- Asking questions that are of interest to you—related to things you can do
- Your roles shift away from you as the good student with the All Knowing Professional (informational interview style) to—
- Successful Inquiring Professional (you) trading ideas with an industry professional who shares concerns about a PINT

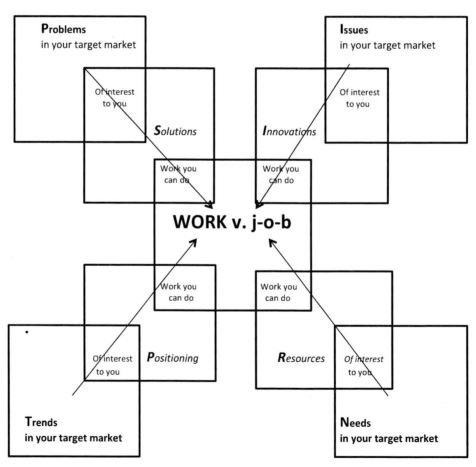

The PINT surrounds work that needs to be done. If you asked a key decision maker if his organization is hiring, he might tell you, "No," or, "I don't know, have you checked our website?" or, "I can't keep track of that. Have you called our HR department?" But your carefully crafted networking questions will create conversations that indicate work that needs doing. That's when decision-makers take notice. Depending on their level of authority, they start to think about creating a job because the right talent (you) just made them realize that now is the time to act.

And here's the power of network-driven research when you're a SIP with a PINT: it puts you in touch with work that needs to be accomplished—not just jobs that need to be filled. Some examples will help you see how successful, inquiring professionals have focused their inquiries into the segments of the market that were of interest to them by conducting a PINT Analysis and offering solutions, innovations, resources, and positioning ideas.

As a SIP with a PINT, You Can Move Out

The Aspiring Entrepreneur. Nathan was always starting conversations with intriguing questions. People often found themselves swept into fascinating conversations with him because he was always interested in others and didn't have to start by telling his own story to engage people. But he always had something personally relevant to contribute to the discussions, and this is how he seemed to guide himself to interesting work.

After a great twenty-two year run in the telecommunications industry—starting out as a technician, moving into fleet management, and winding up in product marketing—Nathan wanted to connect to work that had always fascinated him during his years of business travel: the hospitality industry. His hope had been to someday transition into owning and operating a bed and breakfast as he approached his early to mid sixties.

When Nathan first started working with me he was a bit apologetic about this hospitality interest and goal. "Who in the B&B business would talk seriously to a telecom geek about how to get into their business?" he asked. "I don't have any skills or experience in their line of work. They'll think I'm presumptuous."

I suggested to Nathan that his career research would be better served if he positioned himself as a:

- Successful, inquiring professional with a focused inquiry—rather than a "telecom geek" just poking around asking some "wannabe" questions.
- Person who is well grounded in some of the problems, issues, needs, and trends in the B&B industry and wanting to know more—rather than "a guy asking, 'gee, wow' questions."

With that new frame of mind, Nathan began by accessing publicly available information about the B&B business through industry newsletters, books, websites, hospitality research, and the Cornell University School of Hotel Administration. The goal was:

First, to research the PINT:

- Problems
- Issues
- Needs
- Trends

...in the B&B and boutique hotel industry.

As in any industry, there's work needing to be done behind every PINT; work lurks where jobs don't yet exist.

Second, to get smarter about these matters by asking people questions that were:

- Of genuine interest to Nathan because they relate to something he *could do* or has done (his actual knowledge, skills, and abilities), not just something he's curious about.

And that's the magic. If the conversation is about something that relates back to skills and experiences that Nathan has, he can participate in the dialogue as a professional peer (SIP) and actually exchange information, not just take it. He can increase the other person's knowledge about some things.

Let's take a look at some of the interesting PINT information he uncovered about the B&B business.

The first three resources that Nathan went to for his research were the same ones any person could access:

1. A college library for periodicals and research from the hospitality industry (especially B&Bs)
2. Websites about the B&B or boutique hotel sector
3. Blogs written by people in the business

Result. Nathan found there were shifts in business travel patterns that were starting to favor smaller, intimate hotels and B&Bs. Business travelers were tiring of the big-box hotels and wanting something more personal and homier as they stayed in town for projects or assignments that lasted for a week or two. Trade magazines told the upbeat story, but the blogs told the dirty little secrets about what wasn't working so well—and that's what turned out to be a goldmine for Nathan.

Remember, he was a telecom geek with twenty-two years of managing a fleet of different service vehicles while fixing, installing, and consulting about all things electronic. Take a look at his Focus of Inquiry and the PINT Analysis he did on the B&B business.

Case Study
Sample Focus of Inquiry:
Moving from Telecom to Hospitality

THE FOCUS OF INQUIRY...INFORMS & POSITIONS YOU

These items (PINT) help you build your **Focus Of Inquiry**. Others in your network will help you learn about these topical areas in your market. Behind each of these topics is work that needs to be done—but maybe not yet in the form of a j...o...b.	**Focus of Inquiry.** You can create and offer the ideas you learn from your **Focus of Inquiry** to your contacts and be perceived as a source of help—such as a consultant/employee—and more of a peer than a "student of the business."
YOUR TARGET MARKET (*hotel/B&B*) HAS: PINT	YOU CAN DISCOVER AND OFFER: SIRP
PROBLEMS Local B&Bs can't afford vans and are typically not close to airports.	**S**OLUTIONS Using his fleet management experience, help structure a partnership of B&Bs that could operate a van.
ISSUES B&B preferences for the twenty-nine to forty-year-old business traveler are shifting rapidly.	**I**NSIGHTS This age group consistently chooses hotels with contemporary communications infrastructure.
NEEDS B&B industry needs reservation speed and efficiency while maintaining charm. And lose those antique phones.	**R**ESOURCES He has experience with small biz telecom and reservations systems.
TRENDS Extended time on remote project assignments leading to more business use of B&Bs for extended stay.	**P**OSITIONING IDEAS Segment biz publications for ideally targeted ad space.

Write Now Exercise
Create Your Focus of Inquiry

It's essential to have a Focus of Inquiry even if you are not looking for work. Why? Your career vitality depends on it. Remember a vital career:

- Requires communication outside the organization where you work;
- Includes skills and work that transfer to other industries and organizations.

Staying curious and inquisitive about other peoples' work and organizations will keep you aware of new places where your talent can be relevant.

Here are the three steps to designing a practical Focus of Inquiry to guide your networking-driven market research, enabling you to find out where work is lurking in the marketplace.

1. **Design Your Inquiry Questions to:**
   - Help you experience *connection* with the other person and THEIR PINT as well as your SIRP ideas;
   - Be about things *of interest to you* and related to *things you can do.*

2. **Get Market Information Using:**
   - Various impersonal media first—such as websites, trade journals, professional associations, industry newsletters, and stock analyst reports (don't reveal your most naive state to key contacts);
   - People/contacts who give you insider (not public relations-type) information;
   - Top contacts inside target organization who are well placed to help make hiring decisions—perhaps about you.

Exercise continues, keep reading

> 3. **Your Goal:** Create a conversation that educates you and potentially trades information, enabling you to uncover opportunities where you can offer what you see on the right side of the chart (SIRP) on page 166— the resources for the implied work that needs to be done. **Position yourself as a resource, not just a receptacle for information/ideas.**

A Networking Dialogue Using a PINT

Due to his PINT research, Nathan's conversations consciously targeted two areas (telecom infrastructure and airport transfer transportation) that were relevant to the B&B operators. His discussions also referenced his own interest and work experience to show his usefulness to his target market.

Nathan used a couple of opening sentences when calling or being introduced to a hospitality professional/B&B owner:

1. *"This is Nathan Banner calling, and I wondered if I could speak with the owner, Bill Conrad. Hi, Bill, I'm so glad I caught you. Bill, I've been talking with folks like yourself who are owners of B&Bs about a few trends in your business that also relate to my background and interests in the telecom business. Ellen, the owner of the Lion and the Rose Hotel, suggested you might be able to share a few ideas with me. Is this a good time to talk?"* (At this point, if it was a good time to talk, Nathan would just mention an example of a trend or issue and ask if Bill could meet with him for twenty minutes. The goal was to meet and talk personally. Nathan was looking to build trust and familiarity with people in the business.)

If he had to leave a message, it sounded something like this.

2. *"This is a message for Bill Conrad. Bill, my name is Nathan Banner. In a recent conversation with your colleague, Ellen Meyers,*

at the Lion and the Rose Hotel, I'm afraid she condemned you to the fate of 'expert.' Actually, she was sharing her perspectives on a couple of current trends and issues in the hotel business that relate to my interests, and she suggested you might have a valuable perspective to share with me. I'll call back to tell you more, and hope to schedule a time we could meet briefly to talk."

Results? B&B operators were thrilled to meet someone who understood their needs and also the mysterious world of telecom/Internet connections. These conversations positioned Nathan as a bit of an advisor and also an "idea guy." Let's look at the pathway of opportunities that enabled Nathan to explore this new career space quite successfully:

1. Nathan got one of the B&B owners hooked up with a vendor who was able to convert the period-appropriate antique phones to ones that could accommodate speaker functions as well as high-speed Internet connections.

2. He suggested a way that six B&Bs could structure a shuttle van service from the airport, and not go broke doing it.

3. This led to one of the B&B operators asking Nathan if he would be interested in filling in as a "B&B babysitter" to run the place for five days while the owner traveled to a family wedding on the other coast.

4. Nathan started being handed around as the preferred provider of "B&B babysitting" services. Each assignment was another training class for him, preparing him for his own business and offering him a way to compare and contrast best practices.

5. When one of the six B&B owners got ready to sell her operation, guess who she called first to offer a discounted price without the need for a real estate agent?

The three keys to his success were:

1. He requested brief opportunities to meet IN PERSON and DIALOGUE with the owner/operators. He didn't ping pong emails back and forth.

2. He EXCHANGED information rather than just extracting it from them.

3. He didn't ask about jobs. He asked questions about a PINT (that was of interest to BOTH him and his contact), and his questions led to opportunities to share stories or examples related to his skill and experience.

The Corporate Move

Nora had a simple Focus of Inquiry and PINT. Her story is more common in that she was looking for another role in a corporate setting. Her ultimate goal was to Move Up in management, but realistically that option was not going to happen by virtue of the small size of the software firm where she worked. Her question was, "Is it time to Move Out?"

Case Study
Focus on Fit for Success

Nora had been demonstrating a rare combination of engineering expertise and leadership skill for some years now. She had made a number of successful moves to various companies in the electronics industry, in each case proving to be a solid technical manager and more. She could *problem* solve and lead across functions on projects or task forces. Her explorations with a career consultant came to an important conclusion about her professional objective: she didn't want just another technical manager job at a different company.

Nora agreed that her professional objective, and therefore her market research, was focused on the career path of leadership rather than engineering. This meant that the *focus of her inquiry* into the marketplace was not to ask primarily about products and what was hot in consumer trends or military contracts. Her best work culture fit was going to require an organization with a measurable commitment to developing leaders. She had to shop for a management culture that fit her.

Unfortunately, Nora wasn't convenient to any of the Fortune 100 corporate headquarters which were flush with well-designed management training programs (think IBM, GE, Johnson & Johnson). This desired shift would require research into the medium-sized companies that were more typical for her local market.

She knew that good networking begins with the *people who know and love you* and it will then rapidly spread to the people to whom they refer. This approach included Nora's colleagues in two different professional associations. Her inquiry included three key questions:

1. From your perspective, what would you say are the three local companies that are best at developing leaders from within?

2. What kind of observable or measurable things does the company do or invest in to develop this strong reputation in leadership development?

3. Who would you suggest I talk with who would have a strong opinion about this or even disagree with you?

Not surprisingly, her search was intellectually provocative —and a bit slow. Her focus on leadership development was not a focus that many of her colleagues had. Most people searched for jobs by functional specialty (HR, finance, marketing, etc.) and/or industry familiarity. Her Focus of Inquiry got them thinking and realizing that leadership development had dropped away as a compelling element of competitive advantage that companies could develop and leverage. They preferred to steal from each other, as if that was less costly.

But Nora had their attention now, and the topic of conversation firmly associated her name with leadership roles instead of her engineering skills.

Nora's Focus of Inquiry was driven by an interest in corporate management roles and the desire to develop that capacity in herself. Her PINT was focused on one key trend: finding companies that were building a reputation for investing in the ongoing development of leadership capacity from within. She constructed three basic questions that shaped her networking conversations:

1. From your perspective, what would you say are the three local companies that are best at developing leaders from within?

2. What kind of observable or measurable things does the company do or invest in to develop this strong reputation in leadership development?

3. Who would you suggest I talk with who would have a strong opinion about this or even disagree with you?

These questions were:

- Of genuine interest to her; and
- Related to something she already did well and wanted to learn more about (leadership).

These questions provoked her network to produce better and better clues—that ultimately led her to a GE Healthcare subsidiary in her local area. The GE culture was true to its reputation, and this local subsidiary followed the same trend of investing in leadership development for those who showed potential.

Maintain Your Focus of Inquiry—
Even AFTER You Have New Work

For those of you who are prone to being:

- "The smartest guy/gal in the room," whether you aspire to it or just sound like you do
- Shy or very introverted
- Analytical without being inquisitive
- Constrained by working in a second (uncomfortable) language

- Opinionated to the point of appearing to others to be closed to new ideas

...you run a big risk. It's the risk of missing your average daily requirement of good questions, and, therefore, productive networking. For the purpose of career management, *not* asking questions can lead to critical, strategic miscalculations due to bad judgment in two areas:

1. *Fit* with your work
2. *Feedback* about the work results you achieve—or don't achieve

Fit. Once you land in your new role, the work in your future must fit who you're becoming, not just who you've been in previous jobs. The questions in a good Focus of Inquiry are what helped you find this new work; those same questions will help you find future internal work and organizational relationships that fit who you're becoming. *This is the networking you do while employed.*

Once you are in the position, it becomes time for a different kind of Focus of Inquiry: you're inquiring into the internal, organizational market for new relationships—gaining understanding and clarity about work that needs to be done. As many people find out (the hard way), the job you interviewed for is seldom the job you wind up doing when you actually arrive in the organization. So, ongoing research is necessary to make sure you're using the gravitational energy from meaningful projects, products, services, and relationships to pull you towards the work that is most timely and crucial to the organization's success.

The PINT is still a very relevant model of what to be inquiring about in your conversations with thought leaders and others in your organization. Their perspectives on the internal and external factors that influence the organization are valuable career navigation data. As you look at the organization's Problems Issues Needs and Trends from the perspective of a colleague/thought leader on the inside, your ultimate questions are still the same:

- Is there mission-critical work for the organization that needs to be done?
- If there is a problem to be solved, how do I become part of the solution?
- If there is an issue that needs to be addressed, can I offer an innovative idea or approach?
- Is there a need for talent, consultants, vendors, materials, capital, etc., that I can fill or offer a resource for?
- Is there a market trend that could serve us, and can I help position the organization to exploit it?

Keeping an ongoing Focus of Inquiry and maintaining a good PINT Analysis regarding your current market and organization is part of maintaining an active network and career management strategy. *One of the biggest regrets that clients express as they start to network is that they have allowed most of their network to grow cold and distant after landing their last job.* Oh, sure, they claimed they would never let that happen because their network was so helpful and generous. But once the new work started to gain speed, occupy their time, and build their sense of identity and security (dangerous), they almost totally neglected contact with all but their most immediate network.

There is a good reason for allowing this disconnect, other than being lazy, busy, in prison, or reluctant. People often don't want to bother others with trivial conversations. They don't want to intrude unless there is something significant or business appropriate to discuss. But by having a contemporary PINT Analysis in process, you always have a good reason to talk to folks in your network. The topics are business-appropriate, and you're honoring the other people's knowledge and perspectives with your inquiry.

People are quite honored to have their opinions or perspectives solicited. And you should never become complacent enough in your work to assume there is nothing left to know about problems, issues, needs, and trends—that others might know more about than you. Put those two facts together and you have the perfect reason to keep in contact with your network. The key is to stay curious about your PINT.

Feedback. You must know how your internal and external customers perceive your work if you are to have a clear, contemporary understanding of your fit in the team or organization.

Knowing how to ask for feedback at work is like knowing how to inhale.

If all you do is distribute information and produce work products in your professional role, you're not inhaling. You need to take in feedback from the environment and people around you—not because they're necessarily brilliant or have better perspectives than you—but because *perception matters*. Their perception of your style and work is the reality you have to live with. You don't have to like it, but you do have to cope with it.

Feedback is your primary defense against derailment and your primary lever for maximizing your strengths. Most organizations and managers are relatively weak-to-avoidant about providing feedback, and this presents you with an air supply problem when you try to inhale. Being adequately supplied with feedback usually requires asking for it. Oh sure, you can wait for the annual performance and development discussion—if you actually get one. In that case, however, you run the risk of getting crucial feedback anywhere from one to eleven months later than you actually needed it.

Creating a feedback-rich environment is your responsibility. It is part of a Career Self-Reliant style and one of the supply chains you have to maintaining yourself. Regularly asking questions about your performance, the quality of your work, and the perceptions others have of your style and fit in the organization is part of the inquiry you must run on a regular basis. **Without feedback to guide you, your career management becomes a substantial guessing game and your self-image becomes vulnera-**

ble to the primitive defense mechanisms you might use to block out or minimize unflattering perceptions others may have. Those perceptions should be your clue that some aspect of your style may need to be adapted.

Write Now Exercise
Whose Secrets Do You Want to Know?

The following chapter asks the third crucial career question: *when is it time to Adapt Your Style for greater success?* This is where your *fit* with the culture, boss, mission, and market— and the *feedback* about how you're doing—will be explored in more depth. But, before you read further, it's time to write out your confession. Go on over to those generous margins and write the names of two work colleagues you wish would take a truth serum and tell you all of their most deeply-held perceptions of you and your work style.

No, you can't just think about this now. You have to write the names.

Why? You have to write the two names so that when you're looking back through your margin notes, you'll notice them and remember the feedback you confessed to really wanting. Maybe you will have solicited it by then. Or maybe you'll just have deprived yourself of that valuable information for some more months.

Questions Others Have Asked Themselves

Get a flavor of what kinds of questions other professionals have found themselves contemplating at times in their careers when it was time to Move Out. These questions come from a range of professionals who have attended my "Three Career Questions You Must Answer...More Than Once" classes. I not only asked them to recall questions they were asking themselves, but also other recurring thoughts, emotions, and physical symptoms they were experiencing.

Key Questions People Were Asking Themselves When It Was Time to Move Out:

- Why did my boss move to another city?
- Why did the senior member of our group switch to another team?
- Why was the structure of this team changed with practically no discussion or input from us?
- Why is our product sales and marketing team not going after new customers?
- Where else can I go if the next logical step is into a position that is filled for the foreseeable future?
- If we operate better when supervision is gone, why would I want to "advance" to that role?
- Will this organization continue?
- How do I get more control of this situation?
- Am I doing work that virtually anyone could do?
- Why does this not feel like my tribe?
- Would I even want a promotion if I got one?

The Following Are Thoughts and Feelings Expressed at That Time:

- Projects seem like they're being stretched out or prolonged.
- It feels more difficult to get a commitment from other individuals or teams.
- My favorite boss and colleague have left. Why would I want to move into their jobs?
- Colleagues wouldn't react well if I moved above them. Should I advance somewhere else?
- I need to get out before "it" gets me.
- There are too many elephants in the room that can't be talked about.

- I've gotten good reviews because my boss likes me—not because of my performance. This is not the real and crucial feedback I need.
- I'm the only one who knows how to do this job in the company, and they're messing with the work.

CHAPTER 5:

WHEN IS IT TIME TO ADAPT YOUR STYLE FOR GREATER SUCCESS?

One of the S's in Success

When things don't work out, when someone is deemed "not a good fit" or "not stepping up to the level we need here," it's often *not* due to any one of these three drivers of success:

1. Knowledge
2. Skills
3. Ability

It's more often due to the big unspeakable driver—the *other "S"*: *style.*

> ## Key Term
>
> **Style** is a particular, distinctive, or characteristic mode of action or manner of acting.

Style is that set of behaviors that is being sought by hiring managers and recruiters when they are looking for "chemistry," "soft skills," or "fit" with the culture or hiring manager. It is very real, measurable, and important. But many managers or recruiters can only muster very vague and non-specific descriptions of how it looks in terms of real behaviors.

When is it time to Adapt Your Style? "Or what? Not adapt? I'm adapting all day, every day," I hear you say. And the truth is, *you are.* **The question is *whether you are adapting the right parts of your style and doing it at the right time.***

It's time to Adapt Your Style if your style is dysfunctional, under-developed, inept, or just doesn't mesh well with others. It's not because anyone is wrong. It may even be time for you to change because you're the one with the most insight, resilience, and adaptability in service to a team of less flexible people that crave convention. When is it more about you than them?

Here is a tough question that we do not ask ourselves often enough:

"What about my own professional (or unprofessional) style might be contributing to my own discontent or lack of success?"

This question looks beyond the more convenient assignment of cause or blame to others around you (even if they deserve it). Sometimes, the only way through a tough or even unjust situation comes from realizing you're not going to change the circumstances that are driving it (such as the culture, boss, market conditions, government regulations, etc.), and the only thing you *can* control right away is your own behavior style.

Case Study
Feedback Saves a Manager and a Project

Jill started by earnestly asking the *wrong* career question: *"Is it time to Move Out of my role in corporate finance?"*

But some helpful reinterpretation of her leadership 360 feedback helped her discover her strengths and recommit to her leadership role. She subsequently gained a significant increase in responsibility to lead a reorganization within the treasury function and, like most change initiatives, it was rocky and painful at times.

In fact, it got to the point that she was frustrated and annoyed with the attitudes and lackluster engagement of many of her team members. Here she was, working diligently for enormous numbers of hours each week, keeping the wheels turning on this reorganization effort—while many around her seemed to be compliant but not enthusiastic.

Having learned her lesson about the importance of asking for feedback, she called upon her organizational effectiveness department to design feedback surveys to measure the real versus perceived notion of what people thought and felt about her leadership and the course of the change initiative. The results showed the need for an adaptation of her leadership style if she was to successfully implement real change. Her people saw her as only interested in completing the reorganization by the deadline. None felt as if there was anyone in management who clearly cared about future employee success. The goal was just about getting to the deadline, they felt.

Jill had become short-sighted and narrowly focused in her communications to employees. Motivated and informed by the feedback she solicited, she was able to adapt her style of group communication and spend more one-on-one time answering employee questions about their future. Her personal payoff was in developing both a successful implementation and well-maintained reputation as a leader who inspired results rather than just demanding them.

It would be great if more people posed this question to themselves:

"What about my own professional (or unprofessional) style might be contributing to my own discontent or lack of success?"

Ask anyone who has ever managed people who were cranky, low on personal insight, or generally dissatisfied all the time. Those managers would love to have their employees ask and answer this question. In fact, ask a manager who has managed you this question! I'm serious.

Write Now Exercise
Who Can Provide Feedback on Your Style?

This would be a good time to wander over to the margins of the book and jot down the name of two of your past managers (who are still living, not in prison, and able to be contacted). Do you have the boldness to ask them for any style changes they wish you had made while working for them?

If your boldness factor is really high, consider asking your current boss for desired style adaptations and the specific types of situations or contexts in which they are needed. Global statements about your style, without including sample situations, are seldom helpful. *Get specific.* It might be a good idea to go out to lunch or breakfast to have this conversation, if you can.

After working with hundreds of career transition clients who are planning their exits or coping with job loss, I reflected back on the rare few (literally, one out of a hundred) who have had the insight and courage to say, "I probably didn't have what it took to do my job at the level that was expected." Employers who are referring an employee to me for career transition usually offer background and a confidential description of why the person is exiting the organization. The sad and significant fact is that the organization's story and the individual's story (at least the one they're willing to tell) about what happened (or didn't happen) are frequently quite different.

The tragedy of this discrepancy between how the parties perceive their work is that it represents a gap or deficit that can drive unnecessary misunderstanding. **This perception gap, if left unnoticed or unaddressed, can lead an individual (you) to make uninformed choices of subsequent work, work cul-**

tures, and bosses. And yes, you choose your boss. When you interview for a job or make a proposal to do work, you get to meet your boss. *If you accept the work, you've accepted your boss in the process —even if your intuition suggests a toxic style that is likely to create tension and disagreement between you and that boss.*

Case Study
A Healthy "No" to an Offer

Of all the professors or university faculty I had coached, Lee was the most chronically employed PhD academic who worried about being unemployed. As a consequence, we worked on her marketing strategy—to keep her well positioned in the market while also adapting her assertiveness and decision-making style for greater success at work. This process would also help her make a higher quality choice of next-job and next-boss.

While interviewing for a new director's position in a health promotion organization, all the clues her radar picked up from others regarding the leadership style of the executive director were negative. Lee had worked at developing a keener sense of her own style and the satisfiers she needed from peers and leadership and she wasn't feeling it here.

Despite loving so many other aspects of the vision and mission of the organization, Lee turned down the offer for the position. And within two weeks, she learned that two of the organization's current directors were planning to leave the organization, and that the number two candidate for the open position had also turned it down.

Lee hadn't always been so decisive. She had chosen to subject herself to poorly developed leaders in a number of previous jobs she had accepted—against her intuition. This time, she adapted her decision-making values and style. Yes, people really can choose to shift their values without it meaning a harmful, moral compromise. It's an adaptation. With the help of her coach, she reflected on lessons learned and took this potential job offer as an opportunity to adapt her style of decision making and job-offer evaluation. As a result, she was on to the next, healthier choice.

When performance or fit issues emerge, neither the individual's story nor the organization's story is 100 percent correct. It's never *just them* or *just you*. Both sides have perceptions of the situations they experience, and the perceptions of all the players need to be combined for the most rational picture of what happened. Both sides had some explicit (and probably a bunch of implicit) expectations about what the other was going to do to fix things, and most of those actions never happened.

Unfortunately, the stories seldom get combined for maximum understanding, even at the point the individual is planning to leave the organization or may have just departed. At that point, everyone is rushing to put everything behind them—including lessons that could foster future success.

The Morning After

The key time to ask for feedback is...the day after you start a new job. Ask everyone who interviewed you to tell you what they perceived about you from the interviews. You're the winner of the position, so they're going to tell you mostly good stuff. You may have to specifically ask for the perceptions of your not-so-strong areas. Once you've started this habit of asking for others' perceptions, you have a distinctly higher chance of:

- Finding it easier to ask in the future (a valuable habit);
- Knowing when it might be time to Adapt Your Style for greater success in your coworkers' eyes.

Success: If Only We Knew What That Was

If I knew, I would tell you. There is an entire business book publishing industry built around trying to make success understandable and accessible to readers. Every year, hundreds of authors try to help people define success. I believe there are very personal components or parts of the definition that you must understand before you can determine your personal meaning of success.

I've seen many clients suffer when they create a superficial (and fragile) sense of satisfaction and success by compartmentalizing operational, day-to-day success and defining it separately from longer-term career success. It's quite possible to be successful on a day-to-day basis and allow your operational busyness to blur your vision of the bigger career picture that is not building a sense of success.

Let's start with the belief that there is no single, static definition of success for you, me, or anyone. It's like the weather. We all know the components we measure that add up to weather: precipitation, temperature, humidity, wind speed, etc. But we don't all share the same definition of "good weather" or "a perfect day." Just ask a surfer and a snow boarder to compare their definitions of what a good day looks like. Good luck finding a workable, shared definition of a good day there...Dude.

At the most basic level of defining success, we might start with our definition of our work/job components. Much like defining weather by its components (temperature, humidity, etc.), we can superficially define *work* by the classic terms of *job* requirements seen in most position descriptions. These are the requirements for success sometimes referred to as KSAs:

- **Knowledge.** Information you know that informs your actions (such as German vocabulary words you've memorized, recipes you know, regulations you're aware of, etc.)
- **Skills**. Specific things you can do, such as:
  - Read German text;
  - Write in Arabic;
  - Sauté shrimp;
  - Drive a forklift.
- **Abilities.** (Here's where it gets complex) your capacity to use skills to achieve useful outcomes or business results such as when you:
  - Interpret a letter, written in German, so that an English speaker understands the content;
  - Write a message in Arabic that can accurately inform someone of a need;
  - Create a shrimp dish that will serve seven for dinner;
  - Safely operate the forklift to stack one hundred pallets into inventory in less than six hours.

These KSAs are where most of us spend our development time and resources—trying to acquire more and more knowledge, skills, and abilities. Correspondingly, this is where most organizations spend their time and resources to create more effective employees. But, it's not the whole picture. Over-focusing on just these three aspects of development is not a comprehensive way to define or build success. Let's expand this model into something more comprehensive and practical.

Interests Intervene Between Knowledge and Skills: Then There's KISA

In a time of emerging talent scarcity, driven more by demographics of Boomer retirements than anything, talent management will become a more refined art than ever. How employers attract, recruit, orient, and manage talent is going to depend on accurately perceiving people's interests, not just their abilities to get work done. KSAs will enable a person to get the work done. **Interest in the work as well as in the culture of people surrounding the work will lead not only to better accomplishments, but additionally to satisfaction, employee engagement, product/service quality, and customer satisfaction.**

This insight has been around for more than eighty years. After "The Great War," E.K. Strong developed a way to better match people, who were returning to civilian jobs, to work—based on the interests they expressed. His work, and that of David Campbell and John Holland, subsequently added interpretive frameworks to the interest assessment tools—thereby enabling us to take advantage of a psychological truism about motivation and interest. If people are interested in a task or body of work they generally:

- Pay more attention and do better;
- Apply themselves to the work for a longer period of time;
- Report a higher level of satisfaction with the activity.

The other big "ah-ha" (or "duh") that came out of the research is the fact that people achieve more of the three qualities above when they are also working around people who share their same pattern of interests. There is a sense of "I get who you are." Yes, this can lead to group-think if not mixed with a certain amount of diversity. But it doesn't take much to recall the energy we have all felt at times when we enter a party, new school, or workplace, and discover people who are interested in the same things we pay attention to or enjoy.

Interests and the patterns they form (the various subjects or activities you like, dislike, or are indifferent about) are another defining force in the quest for success and satisfaction. A feeling of satisfaction, and the likelihood of feeling successful at work, can be the result of *match quality* between:

- Your interests and the work itself;
- Your constellation of various interests with those of the people who will be in the work environment with you.

Here is the expanded way to think about comparing and correlating your interests with people in the work environment around you. You are not necessarily trying to become like them or do the same job they do. The more flexible way to think about and use your shared similarity of likes and dislikes or interests and disinterests is to see those similar others as people who could be your future:

- Customers (those to whom you sell a product or service);
- Clients (those to whom you consult or contract);
- Colleagues (those with whom you work to deliver products or services to the client or customer).

These people who have a similar set of interests and disinterests are like your lost tribe. You would expect to work with them in a more harmonious and productive way than you would with people who don't share this similarity, or with a group of randomly selected people. When the shared interests are not present, the awkwardness or disconnect can be obvious.

Case Study
Out-of-Tribe Experience

Devon had been defined by an uncommon level of skill and comfort with math since the age of nine. This math ability was uncommon in her family and rare in her school class. So, who could resist the urge to leverage Devon's math skills into a college major and career choice? Not even Devon could resist—at first.

After six years in a large national insurance company, she was doing well in account management and policy design—

working extensively with actuaries, mathematicians, and sales professionals. But the work had grown tedious despite the compliments from the math pros and her boss, and despite the generous pay raises she had received.

When we used the Strong Interest Inventory to assess the constellation of her various interests, it became clear where the boredom and feeling of disconnect was coming from. In general, the assessment starts by measuring interest levels in six broad categories:

1. **Realistic:** machines, computer networks, athletics, outdoor work
2. **Enterprising:** business, politics, leadership, entrepreneurship
3. **Artistic:** self-expression, art, appreciation, communication, culture
4. **Social:** people, teamwork, helping, community service
5. **Investigative:** science, medicine, mathematics, research
6. **Conventional:** organization, data management, accounting, investing, info systems

Her primary interests (as opposed to skills) were in subject matter and activities that related to:

- Social endeavors (being with people, teamwork, helping others, teaching or training);
- Business and risk (selling, managing, entrepreneurship, influence);
- Artistic themes (self-expression, writing, art appreciation, culture).

She worked with the actuary team for days at a time on major projects that involved working late and in isolation from others—eating few meals together and traveling alone to the client worksite. Her teammates' typical interests included none of the same themes, but rather favored such interests described as:

- Convention (data management, orderly systems, setting up procedures, accuracy);
- Investigative (science, math, performing experiments, solving abstract problems).

Devon was mathematically gifted enough to appreciate her colleagues' work and socially gifted enough to show appreciation. This caused her to be a favored team member; but inside she was starving for shared values and interests. She needed to make the long days and the even longer business trips something less of an endurance contest and more of a collegial experience to boost her mood and productivity.

Her strategy was one of adapting her work style and delegating more so that other account managers had to learn about the mathematical aspects of policy analysis instead of pleading ignorance and leaving it all for her. Eventually, she was able to spend more time in the satisfying and energizing role of supporting her colleagues' work on the sales and marketing side of the business. Guess what department she networked her way into for her next job when it was time to Move Up?

Before you decide upon your definition of success or gauge your current level of success, make sure you're giving credit to the importance of your personal and professional interests. Do they show up in the work you do and the people you work with—your customers, clients, and colleagues? If not, you likely suffer from less engagement, lower energy levels, and less likelihood of producing stellar results.

We need to gauge your interest patterns before we look at aspects of your behavior or style that need to be changed. Changing your interests to fit with work and people that are, essentially, not a good fit for you is a short-term, awkward solution at best. But developing your interests may be necessary as a short-term coping strategy to stay employed with income until you've built a strategic exit.

If your interests are aligned with the work you do and the colleagues and customers you work with, and you still have a sense that success is eluding you, then we should look at and address your style and behavior as the next most likely area for change.

KISSA: "Skyles" Intervene Between Skill and Ability

So success is driven by aspects of *You* that are really about a lot more than the traditional KSAs. Success is more comprehensively defined by Knowledge, Interests, Skills, *Style*, and Abilities. But unless you work as a fashion model or character actor or in some other profession where style is practically everything, you have to *effectively* blend skill and style if you are to demonstrate your ability to do the work and fit in. As previously explained, this blend of *skill + style* is what we call *Skyle*. The way one blends skill and style to great advantage—or disadvantage—determines more of success than we often care to acknowledge.

For Example
Good Delivery Versus Not so Good Delivery

Two delivery men go into a bar. No, really. Two different men are delivering wine to a bar from two different distributers, A and B.

Delivery Man A. *Careful, strong, accurate. Lackluster Skyle.* He carefully delivers the wine on time and intact with no breakage. His strength enables him to move large quantities of boxes quickly. He delivers the paperwork to the manager for all the proper signatures, as he flies out the door to the next delivery.

Delivery Man B. *Careful, strong, accurate. Positive Skyle.* Before carefully delivering the wine on time and intact with no breakage, he finds the bar manager, Maggie, to quickly say "hello" and ask where she'd like the wine stacked. His strength enables him to move large quantities of boxes quickly and stack them where they'd be most convenient for Maggie to retrieve later. He asks if there are any likely changes to her order for next week as he delivers the paperwork for Maggie's signature—and wishes her good luck hosting her son's upcoming seventh birthday party (no wine involved) as he calmly walks out the door.

If you were Maggie, and you were going to expand your wine selection, which distributor would you probably order more wine from in the future?

Both delivery men were skilled, knowledgeable, and able to deliver the goods. But one clearly had a style that made it noticeably more compelling to do business with him. Both were using *Skyle*. One used it to his distinct advantage.

As you look at more contemporary job requirements, you see the elements of professional style and corporate culture being called out explicitly. Consider the following job description for a contracts administrator for a progressive software company.

First the Classic Stuff

Responsibilities:

- Advise management of contractual rights and obligations, and provide interpretation of term and conditions.
- Organize, manage, and maintain all legal documents for the company.
- Act as key liaison with outside legal counsel on complex legal issues surrounding contract negotiation.
- Perform complex analysis of contract situations or data that requires an in-depth evaluation of variable factors.
- Exercise judgment in selecting methods, techniques, and evaluation criteria for obtaining favorable results.
- Provide facts, figures, and other necessary information prior to and throughout contract negotiations.
- Serve as the subject matter expert for questions regarding contract obligations from sales, service, and finance.

Qualifications:

- BA/BS degree preferred.
- 8+ years of relevant experience in contract administration for software and/or technology related companies.
- Proven track record of negotiating successful contracts with clients, strategic partners, and vendors.
- Demonstrated ability to build relationships with internal teams, customers, and strategic partners.
- Proven ability to work with various groups and across departments within the organization.
- Ability to deliver effective written and verbal communication at all levels of the organization.

And Now for Something a Bit Different: Style (Cultural) Requirements

Cultural Requirements:

- **Communicator.** You possess strong communication skills and you enjoy working with customers.
- **Team-Oriented.** You're capable of embracing the ideas of others (even if they conflict with your own) for the sake of the company and client.
- **Driven.** You are a driven team player, collaborator, and relationship builder whose infectious can-do attitude inspires others and encourages great performance in a fast-moving environment.
- **Entrepreneurial.** You thrive in a fast-paced, changing environment, and you're excited by the chance to play a large role.
- **Passionate.** You must be passionate about online collaboration and ensuring our clients are successful; we love seeing hunger and ambition.
- **Self-motivated.** You can work with a minimum of supervision and be capable of strategically prioritizing multiple tasks in a proactive manner.

"Drive and self-motivated"—these are not skills. These describe the style with which this company wants to see you interact and deliver your skills. More sophisticated recruiters and companies ask for this kind of personal insight about "style" from candidates applying for work needing to be done in a certain way.

Beyond just insight about style, recruiters and hiring managers are choosing those talented individuals who can articulate insight and tell convincing examples of their entire KISSA profile during an interview. Your KISSA profile is what the well-conducted job interview is driving to understand. To the extent that you know your profile and articulate it well, you can be a preferred candidate and contributor after being hired.

Style Becomes "Skyle"—and It's Not Always Pretty

> ### Key Term
>
> **Skyle** is what you find when your *skill* joins with your *style of delivering the skill*. It's not just what you can do, but how you do it that creates fit with your job, boss, team, organization, and customers.

We all have Skyles. If we're experiencing success, it's because we've matched our Skyles to the needs and culture of our work and its customers.

That is, we're using our KISSA

Knowledge...

    powered by **Interests**...

        enabled by **Skills**...

            delivered with right **Style**...

                that leads to the productive ***Ability***
                to deliver results.

But there is a hidden land mine that professionals keep stepping on. Needless to say, stepping on any land mine is a career limiting event, but **there is an insidious land mine that many step on repeatedly in their unsuccessful quests for a good work fit: they over-focus on *skill alone* while missing the power of *Skyle* (skill + style of delivering that skill).**

Our work culture and employers proudly proclaim the ability to measure with increasing accuracy an individual's ability to demonstrate a skill. We have structured interviews, simulations, behavioral interviews, in-basket exercises, personality assessments, role-plays, skill tests, and writing samples. They all do a better job of assessing talent than the traditional wandering interview conversation—with the hiring manager doing most of the talking and asking relatively worthless, hypothetical questions.

But even the well-designed and controlled job interviews under which a skills test is administered (such as "Create a spreadsheet to calculate a certain type of analysis," or "Drill a hole of this diameter and depth at this angle into this block of aluminum," or "Sequence the management tasks in this in-basket exercise") usually can't assess the person's ability to regularly produce real work results with that skill. We would need to assess the person with the complexities of the real work context (people, politics, stress, competition, constrained resources, etc.) to have a true assessment or prediction of job fit. That's just not practical in the interview or screening process.

But it gets worse. The assessment/interview really doesn't measure the *style* with which the person executes the skill at work. As a consequence, we run the risk of hiring a skilled person who can't (or won't) match the style requirements of the firm or customers. The applicant, as well as the hiring manager, go on to assume "skills" will create success and sustain that success in the future, only to find out that *"Skyles"* threaten to derail the person. As a job candidate, you may have to be the one who introduces skill+style into the interview.

The over-focus on skills starts early in the interview and screening process for a new job. But smarter organizations are taking extra time to devise better interview questions, incorporate assessments into the process, and train interviewers to do a better job.

As you participate in the screening and interview process, try to create a balance of describing your skills and style to produce a more balanced picture of you. Ask questions about preferred styles in the organization you're interviewing with. If it's a potential mismatch, you want to know now, not after you've rejected another job offer and found yourself four months into a misfit of styles and regretting that you didn't probe more in this area.

Sample Questions You Might Ask:

- Could you give me an example of a work style that would conflict with this team?
- What are some words that describe the style of interaction among team members?
- If you could develop or change anything about the style of how work gets done here, what would you work on?
- I'd like to hear an example or story: either one about a person who didn't advance because he or she was skilled but not able to use those skills in a productive style, or one about a person who advanced because his or her work style was ideal beyond just being skillful.

Your Skyle (where *skill* and *style* of delivering skill come together) will significantly drive your success because it encompasses a more complete picture of both what you're doing *and* how you're doing it. The ability to accurately know and describe your Skyle means you will be able to convey a more detailed and compelling description of yourself during an interview. But this now leads us to answer another crucial question. Regardless of how you describe yourself you must ask, "How do I appear to others when I'm using my skills?"

"How Do I Appear to Others When I'm Using My Skills?"

Genuine, timely answers to that question can make the difference between derailing from a position versus adapting to a more successful Skyle match for your situation. Let's refer back to our discussion of "Elements of a Good Personal Development Plan" in Chapter 3. Creating a feedback-rich environment for yourself is crucial. This means asking for feedback about style, not just skills.

Your organization may or may not use assessments to help you gather feedback. Checking with your human resources or training people is a good place to start to see if these tools and processes are available to you. If these resources aren't available, there is a simpler way to start gathering feedback. Introduce a work colleague to the word "Skyle". It's an amusing, non-threatening way to start a discussion about getting richer feedback. Does it make you just a little uncomfortable thinking about asking for this type of bold feedback?

Write Now Exercise
Time for a Two-Fer

Write now would be a good time to wander over to the margins and write the names of *two* people you could email or call in the next *two* days and ask them for *two* pieces of feedback:

1. What do you recall as *two* of my specific skills that you saw me use? (These observations do not have to pertain to a paid work position. They could come from volunteer work, civic involvement, or military experience.)

2. What are *two* words or phrases you would use to describe me when I was doing each of these skills? (Get *two* descriptive words for each skill, please.)

Now, take out your smartphone or appointment book. Go ahead and get it. I'll wait here. (Insert game show music.) Now, set an appointment with yourself to call or email your request to these two valuable feedback-givers. Oh, and it would be really powerful if at least one of these people is SCARED (Someone Capable and Ready to Express Disappointment if deserved) and able to talk about a negative Skyle that could potentially derail you. It's better to learn about this derailer now—before it actually does anything to harm you.

Exercise continues, keep reading.

So, not only does success have variable and shifting definitions, it also requires that you ask others to assist with its definition—more than once. It's part of how The Three Career Questions operate as a career management gyroscope. The questions are like the wheel in the gyroscope that is constantly spinning around and around. It doesn't spin once and then stop. Neither do The Three Career Questions complete their work after one consideration. Maybe you need to get The Three Career Questions tattoo (or just "3") as a reminder to keep the cycle of questions top of mind.

Success Defined—But Not Pursued

If you know what your definition of success is, does that mean you are *inspired by it? Pursuing it? Enjoying it?*

Ironically, and to the frustration of leaders who have spent fortunes training their organizations' talent, many professionals don't actively develop a strong operational understanding of their KISSA profile. These professionals wait for others to define them, or they focus only on their obvious KSAs (knowledge, skills, and abilities). Some talents are afraid to discover or admit that years of tuition and training have prepared them for work they don't really love. Others are just mentally lazy, not prone to personal insight, or simply interested in staying in a comfort-zone at their current work.

To the chagrin of their bosses, spouses, and children, those who only develop their KSAs—and not their KISSAs—often wind up unhappy and exhausted—all while being the pictures of success in work that pays well and is prestigious, but generates no real engagement and only limited personal satisfaction.

Case Study
Taking Back the Definition of Success

Jennifer was "successfully" pursuing a career in patent law, and was probably capable of making partner in the firm. As a high school student, her math ability distinguished her as uniquely able to pursue a career in engineering with the advantage of standing out as one of the few women in her specialty. No one really took the time to ask Jennifer many questions about this plan and, after all, how could she disagree with all the compliments on her math and science grades?

On the verge of graduating from engineering school, in a horrible job market, advisors complimented her writing skills and research abilities, and suggested law school as a viable way to enter the job market at a later time with even greater employability and earning potential. She got great law board scores, which seemed to clinch it as a good idea in the mind of her parents and advisors.

After law school, she was snapped up by a patent law firm and started making great money working on software licensing and patent filings—all while becoming more and more depressed. Partners kept coaching her. They gave her training opportunities and important cases to pursue. They put her on the firm's management committees to prepare her as a shoe-in for partner.

The components of success were laid out for her. So, her personal reasons for not pursuing the training, doing mediocre work on some of her patent filings, and acting ambivalent about the appointment to the management committee baffled everyone, including Jennifer. It looked baffling until, during career coaching, we went beyond current success and into her past, which no one, including Jennifer, had spent much time thinking about.

During one coaching discussion, I pursued her seemingly casual mention of an experience during law school. We hit the reason for her current ambivalence. She described her pro bono work as a second-year law student—assisting juveniles and their parents in family court. The more she described her capacity to help, the results she got for her clients' families, and the satisfaction it brought her—the more her eyes began to tear up and her voice began to shake.

We had finally gotten beyond the "can do" of knowledge, skills, abilities, and other people's definitions of success. We tapped into the work that was aligned with her interests and intuitive abilities—and came with a greater capacity to produce satisfaction. This new vision of work started to become success as *she* defined it.

Remember:
- You can be taught more knowledge.
- You can be trained in additional skills.
- You can practice the skills to achieve greater, productive outcomes.
- But if your work is not also aligned with your personality, values, and interests—*you're pursuing someone else's idea of success.*

Adapt and Stay to Enjoy Your Success

Let's take a look at someone who really was positioned for a chance to develop and be successful, but was frustrated and feeling blocked along the way. This person needed coaching in how to design necessary adaptations to achieve the type of success that would fit her individually.

Case Study
Queen of Chaos and Lost Causes

Carol's 360 leadership assessment was baffling to her. She felt frustrated by her inability to clearly analyze the feedback about aspects of her leadership style that needed to be fixed. Her coach helped her to see the results from beyond a "fix it" point of view. She began to realize that her feedback-givers were saying she actually had a very balanced style and real potential as a leader at her global footwear and apparel company. But why was she feeling so frustrated in her role as a key leader of a very large change management initiative?

Carol's background and experience in finance, audit, and process consulting had capitalized on her ability to analyze, detect, and identify problems—and describe them to others in audit reports for CEOs, corporate boards, and committees. This ability to see the big picture as well as connect-the-dots operationally made her the intellectual favorite to lead change.

But this is also where her historic knowledge, skill, and ability started to fail her. She was being called upon to deliver her strengths as a leader and no longer as a consultant to management. She had to *inspire* results, not just accurately point to them and recommend methods to achieve them. She needed to connect with people in a different way and adapt her style (away from that of a consultant intervening from the outside) in order to be successful in her new role (as a corporate change leader and ongoing team member).

Among the most powerful adaptations Carol made was her ability to use metaphors in her verbal and written communications. Metaphors capture images that help a visual person learn. Their story quality helps practically everyone learn and retain the underlying message. And their symbolic value keeps people from being too literal—enabling them to interpret and apply the messages to their work (metaphors *don't* work well when describing things like accounting procedures, brain surgery, and instructions for evacuation from a submarine—wherein the literal description is crucial).

But this was not Carol's normal way of composing spoken or written messages. So her coach started to use metaphors consistently in their consultations. He asked her to use them when formulating ideas or analyses. And he asked her to find other people in her life who were naturally good at using metaphors—and really watch and listen carefully to them.

Guess what? Practice and observation started to produce new behaviors for Carol. And as she used metaphors that were appropriate to her team culture, people began to seek her out as a leader, listen to her guidance, and carry and use the metaphors as a way to retain their strategic focus.

My favorite metaphor came during the phase of implementing a massive re-organization and shift to a new business model. You've probably been there. It's the stage that follows after all the design, planning, brilliant thinking, and group hugs at retreats. This is the implementation stage where stuff starts to not work as well as the concept said it should. Carol became a magnet for everyone who wanted something: help, an explanation, a place to whine, and worse. But when we characterized her role at this stage as "The Queen of Chaos and Lost Causes," everyone, including Carol, was able to normalize their current experiences as being a stage, not the end result of all that they had strived for during months of planning. Oh, and the other thing she was able to inspire with the metaphor? *Laughter*—the saving grace.

This case story illustrates the ideal reason to ask and answer the question, "When is it time to Adapt Your Style?" Carol's work and organization were solid and worth strongly supporting. But the organization was experiencing a period of stress, as was Carol, and that required some style adaptations to be successful. She didn't have to like what was happening, but it was worth the effort to adapt her style to fit with the current events and demands.

Contrasting Styles to Keep in Mind

There are many descriptions for the styles that people use while executing their skills at work. The Occupational Information Network (O*NET) is a comprehensive database of worker attributes and styles as well as job characteristics. As the replacement for the *Dictionary of Occupational Titles (DOT)*, O*NET is the nation's primary source of occupational information. This is an online tool offering you a great source of vocabulary for the world of work. It contains many of the words and concepts to describe your skills and behaviors, as well as concepts that describe jobs and work.

The O*NET Content Model is the conceptual foundation that describes the individual and workplace. (See http://www. onetcenter.org/dl_files/ContentModel_DetailedDesc.pdf for more on the Model.) The Content Model provides a framework identifying the most important types of information about work and integrating them into a theoretically and empirically sound system. One of the important categories of information that O*NET displays in the Model is "Work Styles."

Let's embellish this model a bit. The O*NET version shows the ideal or positive descriptions of styles that are crucial to delivering work results. I added an additional column of contrasting styles. By "contrasting," I don't mean negative. These contrasting descriptions represent preferred styles in some work cultures. The challenge is always to determine your preferred style and decide if it fits with the current organization, team, boss, or customers constituting your current work reality.

This is not a matter of making "one-or-the-other" choices. Your style may be a variation of either of the choices you see. The point is to become more aware of your style of delivering skilled work *and* the style required by your environment. We can see the more ideal quality of the styles in the left column of the following chart. But I bet you know people in companies or government offices who routinely operate from the right column, saying, "It's working for me."

If you are currently in a leadership role, you'll recognize the challenging nature of managing employees with a "right column style."

Desired Work Styles and Personal Characteristics That Can Affect How Well Someone Performs a Job

DESIRABLE STYLES Desired or ideal work styles	CONTRASTING STYLES These aren't "wrong," just different. But would they fit where you work?
Achievement Orientation—Job requires personal goal setting, attempt to succeed at those goals, and effort to be competent in own work. Qualities include:	
Achievement/Effort—Job requires establishing and maintaining personally challenging achievement goals and exerting effort toward mastering tasks. (a)	*(a) I get the work done as best as I can and in the manner I've always done it. I'm more accurate working at a consistent pace and sticking with tried and true skills.*
Persistence—Job requires persistence in the face of obstacles. (b)	*(b) I'll ask once but won't push people or deadlines. Doing so just develops bad feelings.*
Initiative—Job requires a willingness to take on responsibilities and challenges. (c)	*(c) I'm willing to take on work if asked, and if it's not outside of my job description.*
Social Influence Orientation—Job requires having an impact on others in the organization, and displaying energy and leadership. Qualities include:	
Leadership — Job requires a willingness to lead, take charge, and offer opinions and direction. (d)	*(d) I observe and make suggestions and will support the consensus of the group.*
Interpersonal Orientation—Job requires being pleasant, cooperative, sensitive to others, and easy to get along with, and having a preference for associating with other organization members. Qualities include:	

Cooperation—Job requires being pleasant with others on the job and displaying a good-natured, cooperative attitude. (e)	(e) If someone is friendly to me, I'll be friendly back. If others go along with my ideas, then I'll go along with theirs. Otherwise, I won't.
Concern for Others—Job requires being sensitive to others' needs and feelings, and being understanding and helpful on the job. (f)	(f) This is a competitive place and softness or "pleasant" may be seen as weakness.
Social Orientation—Job requires preferring to work with others rather than alone, and being personally connected with others on the job. (g)	(g) I'm an introverted analyst and need quiet isolation to concentrate.
Adjustment Orientation—Job requires maturity, poise, flexibility, and restraint to cope with pressure, stress, criticism, setbacks, personal and work-related problems, etc. Qualities include:	
Self Control—Job requires maintaining composure, keeping emotions in check, controlling anger, and avoiding aggressive behavior, even in very difficult situations. (h)	(h) Strong emotions, even anger, show people what I think is important or needed, and help me push back on aggressive people.
Stress Tolerance—Job requires accepting criticism and dealing calmly and effectively with high stress situations. (i)	(i) I'm better able to get rid of my stress if I'm honest about my feelings and don't act calmly and agreeably when I really think things are screwed up or unfair.
Adaptability/Flexibility—Job requires being open to change (positive or negative) and to considerable variety in the workplace. (j)	(j) People here will roll right over me if I don't show them that I've got backbone.

Conscientiousness Orientation—Job requires dependability, commitment to doing the job correctly and carefully, and being trustworthy, accountable, and attentive to details.
 	
Qualities include:
 	
    Dependability—Job requires being reliable, responsible, and dependable, and fulfilling obligations.
 	
    Attention to Detail—Job requires being careful about detail and thorough in completing work tasks. (k)
 	
    Integrity—Job requires being honest and ethical.
	(k) I let people know as much as they need to get their work done, but not so much that they worry inappropriately or gossip about matters that don't concern them.

Independence Orientation—Job requires developing one's own ways of doing things, guiding oneself with little or no supervision, and depending on oneself to get things done.
 	
Qualities include:
 	
    Practical Intelligence Orientation—Job requires generating useful ideas and thinking things through logically. (l)
 	
    Innovation—Job requires creativity and alternative thinking to develop new ideas for and answers to work-related problems. (m)
	(l) This is a CYA environment with bureaucracy that punishes those who get creative or violate established protocols. I stick close to my boss on most matters.
	
	(m) Experimentation can be expensive and poorly rewarded if it's not a smashing success. Be careful.

Analytical Thinking Orientation—Job requires analyzing information and using logic to address work-related issues and problems. (n)	*(n) Just follow the rules and protocols. Other people will take care of diagnosing why things may not go well.*

It's easy to see how people can reinterpret idealized work styles and adopt personal styles that are different, a little dysfunctional, and make personal good sense to them. Our own styles always seem sensible to us. The goal is to adapt to a functional style, not necessarily the one that is easiest for you.

Pre-Retirement Adaptation for the Career Home Stretch

Each generation of workers will approach an age-driven shift in their style of working. They run into Skyle issues as they age past, typically, their fiftieth birthday. This is a time that demands self-awareness and career decisions that must be made and executed with great consciousness. Skills are still present, but the style with which they are delivered is starting to look different.

If you are in this fifty-plus age group, or if you have been working with a colleague who has moved into this stage of development, you may have noticed a couple of personal shifts:

- You're increasingly driven by the personal value of *generativity* (caring more about others—those who come after you as well as those ahead of you in their organization or profession). Your legacy and that of the organization means more to you at this stage.
- You are less driven by the newest methodology. You are better able to compare and contrast it to previous methodologies that you mastered or experienced before.
- Your cognitive speed might have decreased a bit, but your comparative analysis and systemic knowledge may exceed everyone around you.

You may be at the awkward organizational interface where "static quality" meets "dynamic quality." "Static quality" is achieved by knowing what to maintain or *not* change from among the methods or thinking that already exist. "Dynamic quality" is achieved by knowing how and when to change aspects of an organization and adapt new technology or methods.

With the American obsession for change, there is often a compulsive urge to change things when new leadership takes over. The sub-optimized mergers and acquisitions of the 1990s (and beyond) were classic examples of failed opportunities to recognize the difference between static and dynamic quality, and know how to balance them. Most mergers were driven overwhelmingly by financial analysis—leaving the values of culture, talent, and processes to be discounted until it was often too late to sustain their benefits. And it was the older worker who was most frequently thrown overboard in the absence of recognizing the measure of "static quality" needed to sustain viable quality and profitability.

At this stage of your career, knowing when and how to Adapt Your Style can be crucial for sustaining your organizational participation in a meaningful way. Your KISSA profile is changing. Your values and interests are different. It makes sense that your contribution will be different.

Case Study
Mentoring in the Home Stretch

Juan's title was "Senior IT Architect" with a transportation and logistics company. He had developed his IT expertise to the level of understanding the esoteric world of middleware in information technology. Functioning at the level of "architecture" rather than building programming or hardware operations, he was about three to four years from a targeted departure from the industry—and a "Third Wave" redefinition of work in his early sixties. And he found himself surrounded.

He was increasingly surrounded by younger professionals with:

- More contemporary training and certifications;
- A relatively indiscriminate belief in technology as the cure for everything.

They loved to multi-task, whereas he loved to focus. They constantly wanted to create teams to work on projects, while he was happiest working mostly on his own with occasional outside coaching or consultation.

Career strategy had become a serious matter for Juan, and adaptations to his style were going to be crucial if he was to accomplish two objectives:

1. Avoid a major investment of time and money to update his educational credentials for what was only going to be a short stay in his current profession.
2. Stay with his current employer so as to avoid a job search and acculturation to a new organization.

Juan had a slight preference towards introversion and was most comfortable working on his own for major parts of the day. His social skills were very good, however, and his ability to read the attitudes, abilities, and needs of coworkers was strong. These were the strengths he could build on to support his adaptation to a new role.

The Plan:

- Capitalize on his capacity to mentor others in their development and build their capacity to act with a balance of judgment skills and technical skills.
- Move to a position that would open in the next year. The position was called "Senior Technical Advisor" and was within the account management function.

The new role entailed working alongside newer, younger engineers who had more contemporary systems knowledge. Juan's new goal was to finesse situations where his younger colleagues tended to oversell a technology solution (and undersell the consulting side of service). His healthy balance of understanding how to blend technology tools with the need for skilled human judgment enabled Juan to coach and spot the talent who could move into either technical consulting or management roles.

There was another major, practical arena of adaptation. Juan needed to adapt his personal fitness, diet, and sleep habits to be more vigilant about regenerating his energy each day. The more extroverted interactions with colleagues and clients most days left his introverted nature more exhausted than a typical day working alone at his computer in his cubicle. The new role fulfilling the title of Senior Technical Advisor capitalized on his existing technical skill while allowing him to adapt his style to develop and coach others. By successfully adapting to this new role, Juan reduced the need to invest his time and money in the newest technology credentials. His exit strategy is possible now, and both the organization and Juan are getting key needs met.

Juan is not alone in his efforts to adapt his work to his developmental and generational strengths. Managers everywhere are learning to adapt their styles to the needs of up to four generations in the workplace at the same time. There are great leadership models, such as the Hersey-Blanchard Situational Leadership Model (made popular by Ken Blanchard in *One-Minute Manager*) built around the central need to adapt manager styles to the people being managed and the context.

Your challenge is to *first know yourself.* **You have constantly evolving interests, personal and generational values, beliefs, and a resulting style that you bring to your work.** It is from this point of self-insight and self-description that you will compare your style:

- To your peers;
- To what your team needs;
- To what your boss expects;
- To what your organization expects;
- To what your customers say they want;
- To what your professional ethics require you to do.

Then you can decide if your success requires you to adapt to circumstances and expectations that are different from how you are today. Again, insight requires that you have feedback. Become your own "environmentalist," and start to create those feedback-rich environments around yourself that produce insight from self-reflection, assessments, and the observations of others. This feedback will seldom happen by itself in a timely fashion. You need to actively gather it.

Pre-Conditions to Adapting Your Skyles: Feedback and Values-Play

The need to adapt your mixture of skills and style (Skyles) is ideally preceded by ongoing, good habits of creating a feedback-rich environment at work. If you don't typically get immediate feedback in work situations, you need a plan to find trusted others who can provide you the perspectives you need to design your Skyle adaptations. *Kids, don't try this trick at home alone.* Discuss your feedback and proposed adaptations with a trusted other. **You'll never know how brilliant or defensive your adaptations seem if you only work them out in your own head.**

When you sense the need to adapt, and yet you observe yourself doing nothing to seek clarification or pursue changes in your Skyles, *it's time to examine what you want/value/believe—not what you're capable of or what others want you to change.* This is also an important time to consider which of The Three Career Questions you are actually needing/wanting to answer.

Are you avoiding adaptations of your Skyles due to a real and fundamental mismatch with your work or the work culture? Maybe you've resigned already but stayed on the job. The right question for you may be, "Is it time to Move Out?"

If you are developing your leadership capacity, the question of Skyles and needed adaptations may arise at a time when you are striving to answer, "When is it time to Move Up?" Your challenge is to:

- Intimately understand the specific requirements of that next level of leadership;
- Gather enough feedback to know what key Skyle changes are required to function at that level.

The absence of this knowledge and insight may be what is delaying or preventing your ability to answer the question about "Moving Up"—and act on it.

The Leadership Pipeline (2001)—by Ram Charan, Stephen Drotter, and James Noel—did an elegantly simple job of outlining the developmental shifts in skill, values, and time management that must occur when a person is "Moving Up" (or down) to each and every new level of leadership responsibility. Three aspects of your approach to work must be adapted every time you shift to a different level of leadership:

1. Values
2. Skills
3. Time management

These three key elements offer you focus during a time of transition—when things tend to turn into another Tornado, spinning lots of ideas about what to do but making it hard to prioritize or focus.

But just knowing the need to adapt, and having a conceptual model, are not enough. Your adaptation also holds emotional and behavioral components. One clearly needs to be motivated, curious, and willing to risk a bit of hubris to learn, adapt, and replace some old, familiar, and historically quite successful behavior patterns (rewarded in your previous, lower position) with newer behaviors.

If adapting was simple and straightforward, organizations wouldn't be spending millions of dollars on training and development programs and leadership coaches to help talented people adapt their styles. What stands in your way of making adaptive changes called for by changing circumstances, your boss, and even yourself? *Conscious Values Play* may be required.

Values Blocking Your Adaptation

High-quality feedback (about what and when to adapt) and values-play are preconditions for successfully adapting your Sky-les. Values-play refers to experimentation with beliefs and values.

At first, suggesting such experimentation may sound synonymous with promoting dishonesty about your true beliefs or values—simply in order to try new ones. But the fact is, the "truth" that is constructed by your current beliefs and values differs from the one you had in previous stages of your career. As we said in the beginning ("Introduction"), "You successfully transitioned from adolescence to adulthood by making—and then changing—most of the decisions and relationships you had made along the way. This ability to adapt turns out to be an awkward but essential skill that you likely have used unconsciously throughout your career. Now, I hope to help you use it more consciously." The same goes for many (not all) of your values and beliefs, especially about your work. So, let's return to adapting your blend of skill and style for success at work.

Let's start with a premise that you are fundamentally well-suited for your role and work—but appear stuck or stubborn about Adapting Your Style. But wait a minute. **Are you "stuck" in the sense that you *don't know how* and are therefore unable to change? Or are you stuck because you're *defending something you value/believe* but are not consciously aware of?**

For example, Sam, who heads up a project management office at a manufacturing company, might be willing to adapt his style to be more thorough and prepared when leading project review meetings, but perhaps he's not made this change for a number of possible reasons:

- He is a bit nervous and self-conscious about what others would think if they witnessed him trying to change his way of doing things.
- He is feeling a bit tired and hoping to reserve his energy at this time.
- He is a perfectionist who is reticent about experimenting with adaptations unless he can get it absolutely right the first time.

(We'll look at a story, in a few pages, of how a situation similar to this actually played out for an IT manager who was struggling with meeting management.)

If any of these are true beliefs or values held by Sam, it doesn't matter if they are:

- Rational or irrational;
- Socially acceptable or unacceptable;
- Conscious or unconscious to Sam as he thinks about his work style during the day.

The fact is, these beliefs are having a limiting effect on his ability to adapt. They represent the subtle stopping forces that keep him from making the most sensible and clearly beneficial changes to his Skyle. And here's the really insidious part: as dysfunctional as these thoughts or feelings may appear, they are as likely to have evolved from his strengths as from his weaknesses.

Returning to the example of Sam, our manager who needed to lead project review meetings differently, we see a man suffering from two beliefs that previously made him successful as a manufacturing engineer:

1. Troubleshooting is the ultimate art of brilliant engineers, like me.
2. Be Mr. Reliable, and stay the same so that people continue to trust and rely on you.

As a proven troubleshooter, Sam has come to rely on this ability to sweep in at a minute's notice and see the way through a production manufacturing problem. Relying on that in-the-moment talent, Sam hasn't needed to spend time preparing for meetings ahead of time. He just swoops in and saves the day.

Sam believes he was promoted early because of his "Mr. Reliable" character. His approach, demeanor, and style of interaction were always the same, and his boss found him easy to manage and promote. Sam didn't want to mess with success by suddenly becoming a different type of person.

With these competing beliefs pushing back on sensible feedback from his boss and a colleague stating that he could "be better prepared for these project review meetings that are consistently running too long," Sam has stalled. He's not adapted his style to the needs of the situation. There's a very strong chance that he isn't conscious of his competing beliefs and values. He'll need to become aware first, and then try some different beliefs and thoughts to see if he can comfortably get out of his own way.

Let's look at a process for assessing and becoming aware of

these embedded beliefs. This method and the steps you'll see will most likely require dialogue with a *trusted other* to help you (or someone like Sam) hear some of the embedded beliefs or thoughts about the challenge to change.

Rationally Adapting Values and Beliefs

Cognitive psychologists have long understood the potential of beliefs to block us from taking actions that would be in our own best interest or would help minimize emotional upset. They have taught us to be vigilant about the use of such words as "should, ought to, supposed to," for they often are clues to underlying beliefs or values that are not grounded in any real world rationality. These irrational beliefs or values trigger emotions or actions that are not based on our actual, rational circumstances and, therefore, not usually in our best interests.

Let's look at a couple of examples of the ABCs of some irrational beliefs and values. We'll look at three elements to each vignette, and see how to reframe them for a more manageable, personal reaction. Here are the definitions to use in the ABC analysis of each situation:

A = **A**ctivating event—something that happens

B = Irrational **B**elief or value that you tell yourself is "true or important" about this event

B+ = Beliefs that are more rational than others

C = **C**onsequential and often intense feelings or perceptions that stem from holding your beliefs

C+ = More rational and less intense emotional reactions or perceptions that stem from a more rational set of beliefs

Scenario #1
Leading Change

A (Activating event) = You are an executive leading a change initiative to switch from an organizational structure designed around product lines to a structure based on customer groups. The change is slow and uncoordinated due, in your opinion, to ineffective middle management.

B (Irrational belief or value) = You believe, "Managers should be able to follow such a clear strategy and get on board with the company's change initiative. Things are moving slowly because they probably have some foolish hidden agenda."

C (Consequential feelings or perceptions) = You feel, "These managers are not the brightest and obviously can't be trusted. They're trying to sabotage me. Where's that bottle of antacid tablets?"

Scenario #2
Skipped Over for Promotion

A = You are approaching fourteen years with the company, and the promotion of one of your less senior colleagues has just come to your attention.

B = You believe, "I should have made vice president by now. Loyalty and hard work need to be recognized."

C = Your perceptions include, "I feel cheated. My trust for the CEO is at a new low."

The beliefs stated above sound like those we hear in organizations all the time. Because of their familiar tone—or because they're stated by someone who is a friend—we often forget to challenge the irrationality behind them.

Let's look at what the same professionals sound like when they are challenged to substitute a more rational belief or value in their thinking. Then let's explore how it drives different emotional consequences and action plans.

These are examples of *experiments* with belief and values—also known as Conscious Values Play. We've spent our whole lives adapting our beliefs about things (such as the tooth fairy) and our values (how important was your "sacred" weekly round of golf the week your adorable first child was born?). Sometimes the changes in our values were nearly instantaneous, but more often they were the result of incremental changes in perceptions due to:

- Suggestions by trusted others;
- Personal observations and experiential learning;
- Objective analysis.

The changes come about due to "thought experiments" that lead to "Conscious Values Play." You need to try on or play with these new thoughts and notice how they lead to new values or priorities. During a dialogue with a coach or a trusted other, you will be offered alternative behaviors and ways to perceive situations. You don't have to adopt and adapt right there, on the spot. Play with new beliefs and behaviors within the Think Out Loud Laboratory of dialogue with a trusted other. Take some intellectual and emotional risks, and experiment in that Think Out Loud Lab; that's why they call it a "lab." Later, when the annoying, real situations come along, substitute the new, experimental frame of reference from the lab (the more rational thoughts or beliefs) and see if you feel better when you do.

Now we'll look back at our two scenarios and how the individuals experimented with different beliefs and more rational interpretations to promote less tension and more action.

Scenario #1

Leading Change—More Rationally

A = You are leading a change initiative to switch your organization from a structure around product lines to a structure based on customer segments. The change is slow and uncoordinated due to middle management, in your opinion.

B = You think, "Managers should be able to follow such a clear strategy and get on board with the company's change initiative."

B+ = The more rational You appreciates that one of your most trusted engineers, who's known you for more than ten years, was brave enough to be both honest and diplomatic with you. She helped you see change management as a skill set the team needed to acquire, not one that was instilled through your badgering and vague humiliation (how others perceived your tone in recent staff meetings). Her frank feedback helped you switch to a more rational perception and approach, stating: "It would be much easier if these managers were more experienced at change management; but the fact is, we didn't hire them for that, and they're not experienced. It would have been better to offer them development in this area before we kicked off the initiative."

C = Initial consequences and conclusions, "These managers are not the brightest and obviously can't be trusted. They're trying to sabotage me. Where's that bottle of antacid tablets?"

C+ = Your *new* more rational conclusion is, "I hired most of these managers because of their skill and experience as product-line managers. They're struggling to handle this 'change management' curve ball I've just thrown them. I'll consult with our training and development people for the resources needed to boost the team's performance."

Scenario #2
Skipped Over for Promotion—Rationally
A = You are approaching fourteen years with the company, and the promotion of one of your less senior colleagues has just come to your attention.

B = You think, "I should have made vice president by now. Loyalty needs to be recognized."

B+ = Rational You thinks, "It would have been nice to make VP in this last quarter. My colleague has delivered results pretty quickly with his international knowledge. Since the company is moving toward more global markets and away from my strength in domestic markets, he's got both future as well as current potential to deliver results."

C = Your perception includes thoughts like, "I feel cheated. My trust for the CEO is at a new low."

C+ = You say to yourself, "I feel disappointed. Hopefully I'll make VP within the next year. I need to actively pursue international market knowledge and definitely schedule time for building more trust with the CEO. I've let myself drop off her radar."

The above examples are quick demonstrations of how to convert the "should and ought to" thinking into new interpretations that can lead to less anxiety and more constructive action.

Now let's consider a more detailed example of style adaptation and get into the head of a professional who is managing his career. We want to check for the type of conflicting *beliefs* or *values* that might be blocking his adaptation to a more successful style of handling a leadership role.

Case Study
Good Suggestions—But No Action

The feedback had come to Don, the IT director, from a couple of credible sources: peers and his boss. They said, "You're spending too much staff time in poorly-planned project review meetings."

Don *said* he was willing to adapt his style to be more thorough and prepared when leading project review meetings. It was obviously a good idea. This was a pretty obvious Skyle that he had pledged to change about two months ago:

- Skill = Leading teams to consensus on actions to be taken
- Style = Being flexible and open during review meetings to discussions about everything and anything

- Skyle (blend of skill + style of delivery) = Managing meetings so that they foster communication but do so clearly and efficiently for all

Still, information that he should have communicated in a memo was being announced in Don's friendly, rambling, conversational style. And, consensus building that should have been done in a staff or planning meeting was using up too much time in project review meetings.

He had said he was willing to change. Clear changes were suggested to him—but so far, nothing happened.

When Don talked to his coach about the lack of progress toward change, here's what they uncovered as underlying beliefs acting as mysterious, competing forces and preventing him from adapting his approach for greater success:

- Don was a bit nervous and self-conscious about what others would think if they perceived him as conspicuously trying to change his way of doing things.
- He was feeling a bit tired and hoping to just get by at this time. He was working on a better life balance after some negative test results from his naturopath and the repeated concerns expressed by his wife and daughter.
- Don was a perfectionist and always reticent about experimenting with adaptations. He only wanted to experiment if he could get it right the first time.

These countervailing values or beliefs about what was important were not really conscious in Don's mind. In coaching, we discovered them only by asking lots of questions and by starting with the notion that thoughtful, self-protective (if irrational) beliefs were blocking him. These were not wild, crazy, or ignorant ideas—or angry, defiant desires to sabotage himself or others.

Here's what was blocking Don's adaptation to a new style:

- He simply had competing sets of beliefs.
- Each belief was powerful enough, whether conscious or subconscious, to counteract the suggestions for change and, consequently, prevent action—even for his own benefit.

Adaptation and success came as we substituted more rational beliefs or values for the ones that were competing with each other and preventing adaptation.

Good Suggestions Combined With a Values Clarification to Kick Start Action

- **A** (Activating event) = Don has been told that project review meetings have to be conducted more productively.
- **B** (Not so rational belief) = He thinks, "My team is going to wonder what's wrong when I change my style. Changing is okay, but only if I get it right on the first try."
- **B+** (More rational beliefs to substitute) = He thinks, "My team needs to change style. I might as well model it by going first. I'll explain that I'm 'experimenting over the next few weeks' to adapt our meetings and my leadership style so we use meetings more effectively."
- **C** (Consequence that stems from irrational beliefs) = He feels, "I better think about this some more and not institute the change until I've got a 'bullet proof' change strategy that won't make me look unsure and destabilize the team."
- **C+** (More rational idea to substitute) = He feels, "Experimenting with better ways to conduct meetings gets them AND me on the road to adapting. It can promote more team involvement. I don't have to get it right the first time, and they won't be expecting perfection if we're 'experimenting.' This feels doable."

Keep in mind the value of involving a trusted other for insights like these. Our examples are clear and simple, but real work-life often isn't. Your beliefs are often running in the background—your subconscious. Until you get introspective and objective about these matters, you're likely to miss some of the less-than-rational beliefs that motivate your Skyles. How will you uncover these values and beliefs and create needed experiments in Conscious Values Play?

Write Now Exercise
Change Your Skyle

It's time to move on over to those generous margins and give yourself a decent answer to the question of "how." Jot down the name of one person with whom you could discuss a part of your Skyle that seems stuck in a less than ideal mode. Also, describe your undesirable Skyle in your notes too. You wouldn't want to find someone's name written in the margin for seemingly no reason, would you?

Now, do *you* have any competing beliefs that would keep you from contacting this person for a dialogue about this matter? That's right, write 'em down over there.

When Strengths Become Weaknesses

First, let's mention where weaknesses fit into your KISSA profile. They can be assessed and self-diagnosed in many cases. Additionally, as you know, many people are willing to help you become aware of what's not working, at least from their perspectives. To the extent we come to know our weaknesses, through insight or feedback from others, we gain another piece of the puzzle that shows us where, what and how to adapt.

As most managers know from conducting performance reviews, many people are far more critical of their own performance than others are. Our culture promotes the "constant critic" who is looking for improvements in himself and others. But knowing about a weakness and doing something about it—or adapting often involve two very different states of mind. The first act is more intellectual and can take place totally in your head: that is, "knowing." Doing something about it requires a plan for practicing new behaviors and sticking with them long enough to create a new habitual style.

The most ironic weakness is one that combines a skill you're good at and a style that causes you to overuse that skill. This is when a strength becomes a weakness—one of the hardest to self-diagnose and change because it originates from a quality that initially brought you praise and reward.

As discussed earlier, The Center for Creative Leadership, in Greensboro, North Carolina, has long ago identified this phenomenon as a classic cause of derailment for leaders. Their work in developing 360 degree assessment tools to aid development led them to the stunningly simple observation about what caused managers to derail from their developmental path. Let's review from Chapter 3: "When Is It Time to Move Up?"

Here's how the Center for Creative Leadership characterized what accounted for most (but not all) of the leaders in their sample who derailed. It was *"the unchecked use of an unbridled strength."*

It *wasn't* IQ.

It *wasn't* lack of education.

It *wasn't* about the training courses they had taken—or missed.

Let's break down the use of three crucial words in this description. These derailed managers had unconsciously done the following:

- They took something they were good at—*a strength* (such as quantitative analysis).
- Then they over-used that strength without discretion and restraint—the *unbridled* part. (For example, they used numbers to explain or measure things financially, when the issues were related to values or the need for persuasion—and not formulistic proof.)
- Their behavior was unchecked by feedback or coaching because they had set up a feedback-poor environment for themselves. (No assessments or trusted outside source was established to say things like, "You know, in that last problem-solving discussion, you needed to explore some of the ethical issues—not just the balance sheet.")

Let's combine two insights that suggest how we get into trouble with our strengths:

1. Our colleagues, bosses, and work environments will, in the early stages of our careers, identify, reward, and develop strengths that are beneficial to the organizations we work for.
2. We try to sustain our success by using that talent over and over—sometimes overusing it to our detriment by misapplying it to inappropriate situations or using it too frequently.

It's such an easy trap to fall into. It seems almost like a set-up that is designed to "get us." Without the forward vision of a good mentor or role model, it might be easy to miss the ongoing need to shift skills and emphasis. As you progress, it's essential to have forward-looking radar that helps you recalibrate the use of your strengths and overcome weaknesses that will be crucial at the next stage. This forward-looking adaptation is career management at its best.

Case Study
Success Without Development

Alondra, a creative professional in a mid-sized marketing and advertising firm, was recognized early on as quite good at relationship management. Even as she moved into leadership roles, she continued to try to manage the challenges around her as if they were relationship issues—so that she could use the preferred strength that had served her so well in the past.

After a series of well-run accounts and a few turnarounds, Alondra was promoted (not developed—just promoted) to the next level of management. There, she became responsible for a team of marketing and business development professionals. Her new role responsibilities demanded that she have a quantitative understanding of deadlines, quotas being met (or not), and marketing research studies her team was generating.

Much to her amazement and that of her boss (and mentor), her performance review was mediocre for the first time since joining the firm six years ago. And since her boss/mentor was crippled with the same overriding belief that relationship management is the supreme competency, he encouraged her to pay more attention to her staff and find out how to listen to their needs as well as the needs of key accounts.

But six months later, her department's performance metrics were no better—even though she spent additional, even excessive, amounts of time with individual team members as well as her top ten clients. The real issue: Alondra didn't pay attention to quantified, measured results (her weak area), and thus didn't redirect talent resources and timelines to meet client needs. She played to her strength (and that of her boss) and spent sensitive, articulate face-time with key players as a good listener—one of her strongest skills.

Two months later, Alondra quit to join a new start-up firm. Their primary goal, in the start-up phase, was to develop a client base and build relationships: her sweet spot. Alondra did not really develop nor adapt her style with this new move. She merely reverted to an employer with needs that fit her current professional development stage. There, she could continue to over-develop her already over-developed strength.

Alondra may initially succeed in the eyes of her boss or company. Her strength hits them right where they live now. For Alondra to progress in her own professional development, however, she'll need a coach, boss or mentor to help her get beyond reliance on this dominant professional strength—and diversify her abilities.

Conscious Play with Values and Behaviors

For successful adaptations of your Skyles, it is necessary but not sufficient to have knowledge of these values and beliefs that block your way to greater success. Once you have conscious knowledge and insight into the power that these beliefs have to block your progress, you need something else to get unblocked: play strategy. This is the "Play" part of your Conscious Values Play.

Play strategy is an observable, action strategy that describes:

- When you will play with the new beliefs and behaviors (that is, when to experiment);
- What you will say to yourself about the situation that is more rational and productive than before (alternative beliefs and values that you choose to play with);

- Actions and behaviors that you will play with, use, try, or experiment with that are different than your old Skyle.

Children instinctually get benefits from the way they use play. Consider that carefully. They *use* play. Play is a low-risk opportunity to experiment with roles, actions, and skills. We as adults sanction children's play as appropriate experimentation, even if we don't consciously think of it as experimentation. So our kids learn at an enormous pace without worry or blockages to their learning—by playing/experimenting.

As adults, we suffer from a real deficit of non-goal-oriented play, or pure experimentation. Oh sure, we play. More accurately, we compete in various forms of play, and usually do so with the purpose of winning. So learning to Adapt Your Style with Conscious Values Play may sound alien and just a bit illegal or immoral. But, before you call your attorney or a Sarbanes Oxley ethics consultant, think of Values Play as something you already do.

Changing the value you put on something is actually a well-ingrained, common habit. This process seldom becomes conscious because so many of our changes take place progressively, over time. Let's consider changes in your social life. When you found the "special someone" with whom you wanted to spend most of your time, you put a higher value on him or her and assigned a lower value to your other friends (and also perhaps to family, pets, online avatars, etc.). You then started acting on the basis of your changed value by showing up in different places with this new, important person. Luckily, we have a social convention called "dating" that sanctifies and recognizes this process as something typical. This social permission to "play" gives you time to adapt to your choice, and even allows you to unmake your selection and try again with someone new if things don't go well.

But, if you're stuck in your attempts to make a style adaptation (even though you know it would help), and you know what needs to change, there's a good chance you're caught in a values and behavior shift that needs some room to experiment. *Action learning experiments* are often assigned by career coaches when their clients are trying to develop a new approach and need to road-test some new behaviors. **Let's look at learning a new and better approach to an interviewing skill that many dread: describing your accomplishments—without sounding like a bragging egomaniac.**

Here are some of the Conscious Values Play suggestions I make to clients who are trying to adapt their interviewing style for greater success. Many times, cultural or family background predisposes the clients to be extremely inexperienced at representing themselves in terms of achievements and the positive impacts they can make on a business. They have learned values dictating that positive, self-referencing statements are distastefully boastful. So, they limit their self-descriptions to clinically accurate (but dry) descriptions of skills and job responsibilities, with little emotion or credit for achieving results. Their list of skills—using the same dry terms as nearly every previous interviewee—does little to distinguish them from the field of candidates. They find no advantage.

Even when the goal is to describe their hard-won results and proud achievements, clients often report that self-referencing descriptions feel and sound like bragging. To overcome their reluctance to shift their style beyond just highlighting accomplishments, I suggest behavior approximations in low-risk play. First, I gently suggest values and beliefs offering rational, alternative ways to think about making self-referencing statements. Only with these new beliefs in place do we try playing with new interview styles and behaviors.

The sequence is worth noting: consider a new *belief first*, try the new *behavior second*. If we jump to trying the new behavior (because the coach said to try it), we run the risk of having a competing or contradicting belief about the behavior still running in the background. The coachee is simply complying with the coach's suggestion, but not fully accepting the reason for trying it. You need to first rethink beliefs and values to design new and more rational ones. Then, you can try some behavior strategies that represent the new beliefs and allow you to Adapt Your Style for greater success.

Let's return to our work seeker, Helga, who has a hard time telling good accomplishment stories in interviews. I suggested that she use a "client service" frame of reference as a way to re-think the interview situation—approaching it as *helping your "client"—the interviewer.*

First, we need to shift Helga's values and understanding of the interview and the interviewer. Helga is not making a presentation at an interview. Think of the interview as a client service experience. The interviewer is her client who has a task to complete: he or she must make a hiring decision about Helga based on information gathered in the interview. To do this, the interviewer needs to glean information and the emotions of trusting and liking her. Helga's job is to make that task as expeditious, enjoyable, and easy as possible for the interviewer(s). She needs to engage in a comfortable, personal conversation more than a presentation—and give the interviewer what he or she needs: *information and the feeling that Helga is trustworthy.*

The interviewer must be able to both differentiate Helga from other candidates and later defend the choice of Helga as the best candidate—if the decision is made to hire her. With that in mind, Helga will strive to show how she can make the interviewer's job easier.

Second, we identify the behaviors and values that are congruent and acceptable (to Helga) in the context of the interview. The interviewer needs:

- Facts with which to make and defend a decision to hire Helga;

- Evidence that Helga is able to achieve the same type of results and impacts that the organization needs now;
- Enough positive input from Helga to like and trust her.
- Helga needs to adapt herself to the role of serving her client—the interviewer—with information and style that enable him or her to more easily make a hiring decision and defend it to others.

Helga needs:

- Stories, not just facts, about her achievements, because the interviewer can hold onto and recall information if it's in story form;
- Measurable end results that she achieved in each of these accomplishment stories, because measures lend credibility to her claim of making a positive impact—rather than just staying busy at work;
- To feel like she is being helpful versus feeling like she is bragging or on trial; striving, throughout the interview, to be of service is the way to stay positive and likable, and provide what the interviewer really needs without Helga feeling like she is bragging—and thus violating a personal value.

Tip for Telling Accomplishment Stories

Speak about your work results that are relevant to the interviewer and his/her organization. Remember, it's easier for the interviewer to comprehend and remember information that comes in the form of a story rather than a list of facts or descriptors. Make an inventory of your accomplishments stories that describe, for each story, the:

- Situation you/the organization was in when this happened;
- Actions you and others took and your specific role in all of this;
- Results that were achieved (quantifiable results if you can get measures);
- Strengths or skills you used that helped achieve the results

(name them out loud to the interviewer and describe your enjoyment in using them).

Expect this interview style to feel odd, even uncomfortable. If it doesn't feel a bit weird, you're probably not doing it in the full style suggested. This is new. It shouldn't feel easy—yet. But the payoff occurs with the interviewer. He or she will experience the ease with which valid, memorable information and impressions were delivered during the time spent with you. You'll be that much easier to describe and defend as the choice for the job.

Three Stages of Adapting to a New Style

It's advisable to play with some new behaviors in a Think Out Loud Laboratory or some type of low-risk setting. After reading about some of these examples and thinking about your own Skyles, you may have identified a couple of ways you would like to adapt to your current work situation. It can't be stressed enough: think out loud and experiment with new ways of speaking or doing. And start the experimentation in safe situations. **Making these adaptations is not the same as gaining insight. They don't necessarily happen quickly or smoothly. You will adapt in stages.**

Here's what it might have looked like as Helga was trying to get better at telling accomplishment stories:

- **She got in front of a mirror, digital recorder, or answer machine, and started saying her stories out loud and then playing them back.** She was instantly struck by how different the stories sounded out loud—compared to how articulate they were in the privacy of her head. If you don't have access to a voice recorder, call your voicemail and tell an accomplishment story as if you had just been asked a question in an interview or a staff or board meeting. There are two built-in benefits here. When you play it back, you'll hear what you actually sound like on a phone interview. In addition, most voicemail has a time limit (three minutes). You'll know pretty quickly if you've rambled or composed an accomplishment story that was too long and boring.

- **Next, she told the stories to her career consultant, her partner, or a good friend who knew her work.** This friend was someone capable of giving straight feedback, not just encouragement.
- **Then came some networking at professional association meetings and a low-risk interview where she could warm up and practice telling her accomplishment stories.** She was able to hear how the stories flowed or where the flow broke down.

It's only when practiced out loud that you'll know if you're capable of delivering a "customer service oriented" interview in a way that makes the interviewer's job easier.

With my leadership coaching clients, I usually encounter motivated, achievement-oriented professionals who are not used to struggling to learn new ways of doing things. Much of their prior success was based on using natural strengths in the areas of KISA (knowledge, interests, skills, and abilities). They are often working with me on the Skyle portion of their management roles.

I find it helpful to reduce discouragement or impatience for these coaching clients by suggesting a three-stage learning model. Adapting one's style doesn't take place all at once, and the insights needed don't get delivered as a bolt of lightning. The ability to get and use insights and turn them into style adaptations comes in stages, as we see in the next example.

Leading Better in Stages

Lee was brilliant, incisive, and impatient. Her boss loved her. The nine finance professionals reporting to her—well, there was not so much love there. They reacted to her systemic knowledge and analytical ability with wary respect—and concern that they might never be able to give her a thoroughly correct or adequate answer or work assignment that matched her expectations. As a consequence, they were hesitant about stepping up to assertively get their work done in a timely way, and Lee was working way too many hours following up on delayed projects and assignments.

Two irrational beliefs emerged as drivers of this frustrating pattern of interaction. These were Lee's beliefs. We started with them in the coaching process because her own beliefs were the only ones she could control.

1. Lee was an "aw shucks" leader who (irrationally) believed her employees could do what she did because she didn't possess any exceptional abilities.

2. She didn't really value emotional communication, and believed that her employees didn't care about her feelings and values—or about having relationships with her. Lee believed that they, similar to her, just wanted to do good work.

Once she realized the distance and lack of trust that resulted from her intellectual, professional high ground, she wanted to change. She began to see the necessity to:

- Translate and explain assignments and ask more questions to gauge others' understanding of the complexity that she found easy to comprehend;

- Spend more casual time talking about what mattered to her and making her values and expectations more public and explicit, and less mysterious.

To prevent her impatience from derailing experimentation and her willingness to play with new behaviors, I suggested she should give herself permission to *adapt to the new ways in three stages:*

Stage I. Catching herself after an employee interaction, and realize that it was one where she could have used one of her new behaviors.

(Example: After reflecting on the number of blank stares and lack of questions during her process improvement presentation at a staff meeting, Lee realized she was speaking at an inappropriate level of complexity and not asking for questions. She vowed to do better next time.)

Stage 2. Catching herself in the middle of an employee interaction and recognizing it as one of those situations where she should experiment with a new adaptive approach without being completely sure what to do or say.

(Example: After sending a team member a new assignment by email, Lee realized that email would not transmit the importance or context that surrounded the assignment. So, she hit "send," and then walked down to the employee's cubicle to discuss the assignment, not knowing exactly what she wanted to say or how she wanted to say it. But she knew that emailing it would never convey her values surrounding the work.)

Stage 3. Anticipating situations that call for the new behavior; planning her approach; and being calm, aware, and confident while in the actual situation.

(Example: Lee stopped waiting for the perfect time to take the staff out to lunch, and instead just put a date on everyone's calendar. She practiced a few comments that she wanted to make to say thank you to the team for the improved on-time nature of their reports. Once at the restaurant, she was able to express her thanks and be patience in hearing the questions her team had been holding back for a while.)

Once we had defused the overachiever landmine that caused her to expect instant success from herself, she actually was amused by catching herself at each stage of learning and experimenting with new adaptive behaviors.

These are only a couple of examples of Conscious Values Play. This form of play usually produces the best results when done with a coach, guide, facilitator, or someone outside of your own head who can encourage and observe the changes you're trying to make. If Adapting Your Style is difficult, or the process seems to stall, get training or education if necessary. But be sure to check for the values or beliefs (about potential new behaviors) that are in conflict with your proposed change and thereby creating a blockage to your successful adaptation.

Outlived Your Definition of Success?

Key Term

Success is the achievement of something desired, planned, or attempted.

Our operational or day-to-day definition of success—along with some of our values—shifts over time. Our understanding of "love" (hopefully) is going to be different at age forty-one than it was at fourteen. What seemed like a satisfying friendship at twenty-two may not feel like enough when you're sixty-two.

The definition of success in our work shifts with maturity and experience. But without a periodic career check-up or some other wake-up experience (such as a job loss, missed promotion, or organization going out of business) that causes us to consciously examine these definitions, we are likely to run on "auto-pilot," letting the old definitions determine our decisions and even drive our choices about how and when to adapt.

You may have outlived your old, standard definition of success that you had when you finished law school, the military, your first marriage, or your first management training experience. If that is the case, your intuition is probably causing you to have a slight physical reaction as you read this. It is probably time to talk out loud (going beyond just that chatter in your head) about updating your definition of success before you mechanically make more contemporary decisions based on an antique definition.

Shelf-Life of Success Definitions

A personal experience will work quite nicely to demonstrate how this phenomenon played out in my career.

I had to admit to myself that I was pursuing work in a corporate role that was "not me." It was a job that someone else could do better than I was able to. But the new position was offered to me as my old job was being eliminated in a re-organization, and I was anxious, opportunistic, and pretty disinterested in launching a time-and-energy-consuming job search. So, I opted for convenience and got what I deserved.

I took this new corporate staff position in pursuit of success defined mostly by income, security, and expedience. I had been relatively new to the city and its work culture, and needed to choose a position quickly—or so I thought. I decided too quickly based on the offer of a good salary—and then realized that satisfaction was missing as the work evolved over the first months.

The adaptations being demanded of me weren't illegal, bad, or wrong. My initial reaction was to project the cause of all my struggles on other people and their unprofessional reactions to change. My victim role was starting to form. *Not good.* Adaptations were needed for me to:

1. Become a rapid and better builder of political capital within the organization;
2. Or make some bold and painful decisions to move or fire some people.

I wasn't skilled at #1, and didn't like doing it. And, I had to be able to do #1 to successfully do #2 and make it stick.

But for me, the biggest eye-opener came when I realized that adapting my style or developing new skills would lead to a success that *wasn't personally meaningful for me.* I still remember the day that I got unstuck.

After years in various corporate staff roles, my values regarding that kind of work had shifted. I wanted my next work to earn the company revenue and not constitute part of overhead. I suddenly realized I had opted for a role and a set of colleagues and goals that didn't match my evolving definition of success. It was time to Move Out. I was trapped in someone else's work.

As my career consultant had characterized my Skyle, I was a "player-coach." I was at my best when I could personally produce revenue-bearing services while also coaching a team or staff to do the same. It might have been the therapist in me (from a previous career) who didn't experience great satisfaction from building political capital and accomplishing broad, impersonal, organizational goals. I craved being closer to the delivery of service.

I was an organizational agnostic but an interpersonal evangelist. I was passionate about developing individuals and only slightly interested in the corporate goals.

As I soon learned, analyzing one's Skyle issues sometimes leads to realizing that "it's you, not them" who needs to change. Adapting my style was not the best or most efficient resolution of my situation. While adapting my style was what the situation called for, I had to decide if I was going to be a *fundamentally* good fit for the situation to which I was adapting my style.

When I completed my assessment, with the help of some trusted others and plenty of thinking out loud, I was rewarded with two helpful insights:

1. I had evolved to a new definition of success, and it included being a source of revenue to an organizational mission.
2. To my surprise, one of my trusted others revealed that she and two others had passed on the job I had taken because their more experienced eyes could see inherent flaws in the way it was positioned in the organization.

If you've outlived your definition of success, create a new one, or suffer the squandering of your time and effort trying to adapt to the old one that no longer has meaning or motivation attached to it. It may be time to consider the other key questions: Move Up? Move Out? But don't stay stuck for more than six months.

Still Stuck?

If this process of Conscious Values Play finds you feeling chronically awkward or in conflict with your coach's or mentor's suggestions to try things—or you find you're in an ongoing debate with yourself about whether or not to Adapt Your Style to a situation—consider this: You may be trying to address the wrong question (*When is it time to Adapt Your Style for greater success?*).

The Three Career Questions operate as an interrelated set of questions that represent your career guidance system—your internal career gyroscope. As we discussed earlier in the book, the key to using the questions productively is to always make sure you're answering the right question at the right time in your career.

If you've been trying to address the question, "When is it time to adapt your style for greater success?" but despite your boldest and best efforts, your attempts to address and answer it are unsuccessful, consider the other questions. *Maybe you're trying to Adapt Your Style to a job or an organization that is too different from your true Self.* The work/organization may be demanding more than an adaptation; it may be demanding that you be a different person. Don't ignore or underestimate the danger of that demand. Begin to consider Moving Out or Moving Up to a different level in your own development—in or out of the current organization.

But most significantly, don't try this trick alone, kids. Find yourself a Think Out Loud Laboratory in which you can discuss and describe your thoughts, feelings, and values to a trusted other who is both respected by you and capable of expressing disappointment in your efforts, if you deserve it. This work is too important to let it turn into a merely supportive, feel-good experience wherein someone strokes your ego and tells you, "You can be anything you what to be,"—or wherein that same person tells you how inept, misinformed, or misguided *others* are in their perceptions of you. You need straight-talk from an informed observer.

The point is actually to ANSWER the right question at the right time, and take action on the answer. Someone you trust, who is in the process with you, can perform the necessary wake-up call by saying something like, "You said you were going to ask your colleague for specific feedback this week. I'm concerned that you didn't take yourself seriously enough to follow through."

A reasonable response might be, "Ouch—and thank you."

This career management cycle of strategizing your moves up and out, and managing your adaptations of style, is serious business. If you choose to do it consciously (by reading and practicing the contents of a book like this), consider also doing it collaboratively, with a trusted other.

Questions Others Have Asked Themselves

Get a flavor of what kinds of career questions others have had when it was time to Adapt their Styles. These questions come from a range of professionals who have attended my workshops. I asked them to share questions they were asking themselves, but also to recall other recurring thoughts, emotions, and even bodily feelings they were experiencing.

Key Questions People Were Asking Themselves When It Was Time to Adapt:

- *Why can't this person understand my point of view?*
- *Have I tried all ways of communicating I can think of? Are there more?*
- *Have I asked others for perspective/ideas?*
- *How can I succeed wearing all these hats?*
- *What is "success" to me?*
- *Will collective teamwork ever work with my style?*
- *How can I Move Up if I don't know more about _____ ?*
- *Why don't the new people ask me for help or advice?*
- *How do I seem older to gain the credibility with the older peer-group?*

- *Am I being too critical of others because I'm feeling critical of myself?*
- *Is my definition of success different than that of others?*
- *How can I use what I know about other people's style preferences (from the personality assessments we did together) to change the way I communicate with them?*

Thoughts and Feeling at That Time:

- *My "style" seems to be a "hot" issue every time others or I try to discuss it.*
- *It seems like all the successes come from my own handiwork, not the team's. This is not sustainable.*
- *I can't scale myself beyond a certain point. I need others.*
- *My aggressive style pushes others away and leaves me the work and a painful success.*
- *No one seems to want to be bothered to answer questions or offer feedback.*
- *I found out at my going away party that there were all these things I missed by being quiet and withdrawn.*
- *I'm negative all the time, and especially about the leadership team who I barely know.*
- *I'm not going to be happy living the "American Dream." Apparently, it's not my dream.*

PART III:

SPECIAL SITUATIONS

CHAPTER 6:

LEARNING CAREER MANAGEMENT FROM MULTIPLE GENERATIONS AND MODELS

All of us who were working just after the start of the new millennium found ourselves with access to an awkward array of career management role models. Today, we straddle three major evolutionary models of how one finds work, leaves work, creates work (entrepreneurs), and manages a career.

1. **Old Guard (Career-for-Life).** Basically, our hard working parents, grandparents, aunts, and uncles who stayed in one profession or business function (such as sales, human resources, finance, welding, truck driving, or brain surgery) and tried to stay in one organization (such as within corporate, government, or non-profit) for most of the time they worked. Okay, maybe they had to extend themselves to work within two organizations. But the point is, they emphasized loyalty and consistency as core values regarding their work.

2. **On-Guard (Rattled and Wary).** People who are working today and are over the age of forty probably would struggle to name a person who has never been subject to a downsizing, layoff, or job elimination due to a merger, acquisition, or shut down—unless that person is a doctor, business owner, or drug dealer. Now, drug dealers have other "job elimination" problems—but most folks who were working during the intense economic periods of reorganizations and acquisitions got used to losing their jobs and looking for other ones (which frequently looked a lot like the previous ones).

   Over time, these workers became wary of employment in large organizations because such employers were often inefficient and reactive to customer and market swings in ways that would bring on another downsizing. They passed this wariness on to their children and cautioned them about *living to work*, or trusting that a job could last very long.

3. **Vanguard (Permalancing).** This involves working as if one is self-employed. This may be the leading edge model of career management for now, but rest assured, it will become the Old Guard of the future because, as we all know, everything changes over time. Who knows? We may evolve into a future era wherein super-corporations or governments are the mega employers of most people, and we adapt by becoming "organization men and women" as was the case in the US in the 1950s and 60s. But for now, think more entrepreneurially.

The evolving model of how work is defined and packaged is part of what drives the emergence of different perspectives on how to package one's talent. New professional identities and roles, such as permalancing, evolve as a result of the loss of employment security and predictability. Driving much of that is the shift to projects and away from enduring jobs and products that are expected to be valued by the marketplace for long periods of time.

Moving From Permanent Products to Permanent Project Mentality

The 1990s were replete with reorganization. There was right-sizing within certain departments or functions and right-sizing of whole businesses. But this was also a time focused on process improvement within many manufacturing and high-tech companies. As a consequence of looking at processes and the rapid change-out of products, organizations and private industry learned how to package work differently. Our work culture began to "projectize" things.

We stopped thinking of everything we did or made as being needed forever. We stopped associating the work as being part of an ongoing function or department with layers of expertise and management. We started to package work as:

Projects that needed *talent* that could produce *results.*

This shift didn't necessarily bring with it the need to create jobs as much as an **arrangement** with **individuals** who could produce needed end **results.** This arrangement would last for the period of time that the product or service was viable in the market; after that, all bets were off. This de-jobbing of America has led to a record number of workers repackaging their talent—by choice or necessity—as they redefine themselves as and find real work as temps, contractors, consultants, freelancers, permalancers, or criminals.

Lessons from Three Career Strategy Paradoxes:

Paradox 1: The Awkward Trade for Loyalty

The newer, younger, and more insightful workers (of any age) in this new millennium are thinking and acting on Moving Up, Moving Out, or Adapting Their Style on a much more frequent and career-self-reliant basis. They're thinking about the market and acting as if they're self-employed, whether or not they are.

This has many implications for workplace dynamics and relationships. But suffice it to say, managers and their employees have to consciously manage themselves differently than they did during the "Old Guard" or "On-Guard" eras. This new work culture requires all parties to have a higher degree of skill in managing a paradox. We must simultaneously keep both loose and tight bonds to the work we do and the people we work with.

Managers who were used to reaching out with firm handshakes to draw employees into working relationships with the organization now notice that many new recruits are joining with one hand wrapped around the handle of their career rip-cord; they can't shake hands because they're ready to pull and go if they don't like the opportunities they see within the organization. How can this manager shake that hand? He or she will need to lead in new ways and adapt styles of motivating and coaching these newest employees.

What about the new employee who looks out for himself and his own development—while keeping his knees bent and ready to make a quick and easy move to a different job? That person will notice something paradoxical too. If he's going to add responsibility, complexity, and interesting challenge to his work, he is going to have to make a commitment and form a tighter bond with the leaders who are committed to and in charge of the organization.

Paradox 2: Relationship to Technology

Whether you're an individual contributor or a manager, there is an equal opportunity trend that will affect us all in the way we manage our careers over our lifetimes. *That trend is the use of technology.* Again the paradox of loose and tight bonds comes into play. Most workers and leaders will only be able to do their jobs if they are tightly bound to staying current with technology tools. But there is the corresponding caution not to become inextricably married to any one method, technology, or tool for such a long time that your work goes away if that technology dies. In the face of ever greater reliance on technology tools, an individual's conspicuous ability to demonstrate insights and use problem-solving skills will be more in demand than ever. For all who are trying to progress, it will be increasingly important to demonstrate the capacity to do what software and robots cannot do.

Paradox 3: Insight Versus Knowledge— Caution Needed

A career caution: as information technology increasingly takes over the more simplistic, analytical, calculating, and even rational functions of our personal and business decision-making and reasoning, we're left with a new standard of human usefulness and value. It's not what it used to be. It's no longer about having a command over processes. It no longer involves merely controlling information or finding it. Instead, it brings the capacity for insight, creativity, and innovation.

If you're not prone to insight (for example, the ability to look into yourself AND OTHERS and understand who you are in the physical, psychological, and spiritual realm around you) you're rapidly becoming a Twenty-First Century illiterate. Wake up. Technology tools are doing the rest of your work. But, the technology can't (yet) innovate as well as the context-savvy human consciousness; and it can't generate insight into me or you as well as a sensitive human consciousness can.

Do you have a sensitive human consciousness? This description does not mean to portray someone who is overly emotional, vulnerable, or prone to crying and having emotional breakdowns at the sight of a puppy or the sound of the "Wedding March." Instead, it describes someone who can sense how and when they, or others, have needs—and how those needs will influence behaviors.

Are you interpersonally skilled? This means that you can modulate your own behavior to interact with others in ways that minimize conflict and maximize social success.

Career management requires some new styles of thinking and acting—just as our new, emerging forms of work require new approaches. It's a bit like being a contemporary musician. Developing these new styles and learning how to improvise will make you more contemporary and economically fit to orchestrate your part in the corporate, government, or non-profit organization of the future. And, as the music of work changes each year in terms of style and tempo, we all need to be anticipating the change. Like any good musician, we need to prepare to be physically and psychologically adaptive to the new music and how our instrument will play in the new orchestration.

Career Self-Reliance

One of the keys for successfully managing the cycle of a career is to adopt the value of "Career Self-Reliance."

Key Term

Career Self-Reliance is, I believe, best understood by combining two previous definitions: "The ability to actively manage one's work life in a rapidly changing environment" with "The attitude of being self-employed, whether you're inside or outside an organization."

Career Self-Reliance is the name of your future game. As Cliff Hakim so aptly put it in the title of his book, *We Are All Self-Employed*, we're working for ourselves first, and for someone else second. We are striving for employability most of all, not just a j-o-b.

This signals a shift away from a career strategy that is reactive and centered around the job search. Even if you're nimble and able to interview and land jobs after a layoff or downsizing—or after getting crosswise with your boss—Career Self-Reliance requires being proactive and *plan-ful*. It means cultivating over-the-horizon radar, and working both *in the now* and *in the future*. And it means having more than just knowledge about your work and the market you're in. You must develop the capacity for insight.

Sample Question to Assess Your Career Self-Reliance

Here are your first questions to consider. We'll see if you're thinking in a Career Self-Reliant manner.

1. **What is a work-related trend you're watching?**

    Now, really think about this for just a minute. Name a trend you pay attention to.

2. **What sources are you using to check this trend?**

   What do you read, listen to, or watch to keep up on this trend?

3. **What does it mean for you personally?**

   And now, here's the kicker: when you look at your analysis of this trend...

Is it a short-term or long-term perspective? Career Self-Reliance means you can't afford to be too short-term focused (such as only on next quarter's results).

And...drumroll...most importantly...

When you consider what it means for you personally (question #3), are you looking only at **how it will impact you—or at how you'll respond?** Are you aware of an approach to acting on or capitalizing on this trend—behaving in new ways?

In other words, are you prone to proactive strategies or just to reacting (perhaps cleverly) to the actions of others who can impact your work?

The harsh reality is that, over time, the ability to cleverly react to situations (rather than be more insightful and proactive) wears down. You can look nimble and feel occupationally athletic in your twenties and maybe even thirties. But over time, your habit of reacting rather than being proactive doesn't wear well. You wind up losing time and energy to constantly-mounting job searches and reformulating relationships in new organizations—rather than spending that time and energy on progressing with your developmental plan. Again, good career management does not equate to serial job-finding.

Perhaps your goal was to progress into the role of hospital department head. But each time a new technology emerged, you stayed pretty disengaged from it. When it later became the standard, you were behind the curve. So you moved over to a lower-tech area within the hospital—until that, too, was taken over by new technology tools. You wound up losing in two ways:

1. You spent a lot of time and energy looking for new jobs.
2. You stayed at about the same, low level of complexity in your work and got passed over for the leadership role that you aspired to.

The tech tools are necessary to have, but not sufficient to catalyze your progression, in professional fields. Mastering the tools enables you to earn the right to take your career to the next level: being in the arena of meaningful, contemporary work when insights are needed. Your next professional frontier involves being at the place where your insight is needed.

Stay Conscious

So, *Answering The Three Career Questions: Your Lifetime Career Management System* explores your lifetime responsibility of managing your career with the artful use of questions. That is not to say that this is simple, but rather that career management is a learnable, conscious art—and question-asking is a means of discovering crucial issues to guide one's career. Keeping The Three Career Questions in your conscious mind, and in your dialogue with trusted others, is crucial for success. It's your choice as to whether or not to engage The Three Career Questions as an internal guidance system and use them as a sort of gyroscope that never is allowed to spin down and stop. Like good navigation systems of all kinds, if you check it often and never get too far off course, you never have to make huge course corrections.

Keep in mind that career self-reliance is a frame of mind and a value. If you truly embrace and adopt it you will use it to make choices and decisions about your work. In Chapter 5 we discussed the need for Conscious Values Play as a way to experiment with new values and warm up to them through field trials and play that enables you to use the value in low impact situations in the beginning. Career self-reliance is similar to other values that you've adopted over your lifetime. It takes time to play with it and incorporate it into your language, your behavior and your thinking. Try proposing a piece of work that you want to do before anyone asks you to do it. It doesn't have to be big. It just has to be your initiative that launches it.

Take a look at Business Model You: A One-Page Method for Reinventing Your Career by Tim Clark (2012). It will help you start to think like an entrepreneur or solo business-of-one. You may continue to work for an organization that you really like but you will start to manage your talent as if you were self-employed.

CHAPTER 7:

LEVERAGING PROFESSIONAL ASSOCIATIONS IN YOUR CAREER MANAGEMENT STRATEGY

We all do it. We join professional associations as we progress in a chosen line of work, a profession, or an industry. We join because we are consciously or unconsciously managing our careers and trying to progress as best we can. Despite this intention, once we join, most of us find that the topic of career management is never openly or specifically spoken about as part of the regular narrative of those associations. Ironically, we join with career management as a motivation, but then "managing your career" is relegated to an unspoken topic running in the background—all while other topics take up the conscious agenda at meetings, workshops, and conferences.

Answer the question yourself: do you remember any time or resources being spent consciously and specifically addressing career strategy in any of the association meetings, workshops, conferences, or conventions you've attended in the last year? Sure, there were other topics and issues addressed that may be relevant—or which may frame the context of career management. For example, there may have been discussions on technology, legislation, regulation, change management, lean methodologies, etc. There might even have been workshops on job search techniques for those members who had been laid off recently. But, as we've been discussing throughout this book, job search is not the same as career management; in fact, it's far from it.

Why did career management and strategy become relegated to the realm of the "unspoken"? Why is it seldom, if ever, addressed as a topic? A couple of you are saying, "Wait, my association addressed it at a meeting or at a conference." Great, but what about the other 98 percent of you who are still scratching your heads and thinking, "No, wait a minute, we must have addressed this somewhere, sometime. But when?" Well, you're in good company. Nearly all the association members I've surveyed have answered the question with that same sense of consternation. People struggled to recall a time when there was an event, speaker, or workshop that had a conscious focus on career management. No one had trouble seeing the irony in its absence.

So, why does this irony exist, and what should one do about it? We'll look at some of the positive examples of associations that develop a career management consciousness among their members. In addition, we'll look at what you can do to support your career strategy within those associations that are not currently doing anything in a concerted way to support career management. Being career self-reliant means taking initiative.

Why Career Management is the Unspoken Agenda in Professional Associations

It's because of us, the members. In the associations we belong to, we've allowed "career management" to become synonymous with "job search." This means that we don't deal with "career management"; we only approximate it when we're on the verge of job search—again. We're back to equating career management with serial job searching. This phenomenon will come up when:

- We're emerging from high school or a training program of some kind.
- We've been laid off, downsized, right-sized, terminated, fired, let go, canned, eliminated, declared redundant, or just plain lost our job.
- We're in college, and the career center is sounding the alarm that it's time to start working on career choice BEFORE graduation.
- In frustration, we quit a job or organization that we just couldn't tolerate any longer.

- We've come to the conclusion that we don't fit the work we've been doing, and it's time to change careers, not just jobs. But we'll probably over-focus on job search only.

Needless to say, when you look at that list, it doesn't exactly describe some of the most clear-headed, strategically-focused times of our lives. These are times of turmoil and pressure, and we are more likely to react to things (poorly or impulsively) if we haven't been preparing a strategy or contingency plan.

When we enter professional associations and eventually become leaders within them, we bring this less-than-strategic and subconscious operating definition of career management with us. And it determines how we program the association agendas, conferences, and continuing education. "Career management" will only tend to come up during recessions. But, once again, the focus will probably be on "job searching techniques", ignoring the strategic perspective of career management. And, bingo, we're back to reinforcing the traditional thinking about career management as merely finding the next job.

For career management to move out of the subconscious and become part of a more open and frequent dialogue, that conversation has to start earlier, and in a few different places:

- **High school**. Good strides are being made, but unfortunately, school programs are often subject to funding cuts. Also, many classroom teachers have limited experience in other professions or industries. This diminishes their abilities to tell stories that might bring life to the different types of future jobs and professions that exist for their students.

- **Community colleges and technical training schools**. Good progress is being made as community colleges have adopted a broad and practical level of education and training—especially through providing continuing education for employed and under-employed workers. The practical reality is that returning students at community colleges (and four-year colleges) are already proceeding through The Three Career Questions cycle in their careers. They are learning and retraining for altogether new work, as well as getting new jobs. The question is whether the faculty and career counseling staff are presenting this as a conscious, career manangement strategy and process and reinforcing it as such for repeated use throughout life.

- **Undergraduate college career centers**. Again, the focus is understandably on "job finding" and career choice versus career management. In their junior and senior years, students are so distracted—by everything from academic rigor to their hormones—that "career management" seldom makes it onto their agendas. There is a great deal of practical, short-term goal orientation for adults at this age and stage of development. They are anxious about just landing somewhere as they exit school so that they can hope to pay off academic loans and start to make progress in adult life. The Three Career Questions will become more relevant as they engage in subsequent rounds of work in the marketplace. Universities have an ideal chance, though, to plant a model of life-long career management during the undergraduate student's academic experience. This is a prime time to provide immersion in ideas, concepts, and models for how our work culture and the marketplace operate.

- **Grad school career centers**. Here's where it can get interesting. Graduate school is where professionals have committed to career paths and decided to address the "Move Up" question. Essentially, they've started The Three Career Questions process of planning to progress to leadership in their chosen areas of work by committing to their choices of grad school. Here the challenge is to introduce The Three Career Questions as a conscious strategy for sustaining management of their careers AFTER grad school. Many have returned to grad school after bouncing in and out of a few jobs. We want to take advantage of their awareness of the inefficiency of career "bouncing," and enable them to make future moves under greater strategic control. Again, we want to end the concept of "career management as serial-job-finding-projects."

Unfortunately, most colleges and universities don't have graduate career centers that can take a special focus on the developmental needs of students in a post-baccalaureate program. According to the National Association of Colleges and Employers (NACE), less than 20 percent of their eighteen hundred member schools have decentralized or specialized career centers beyond their undergraduate services (phone interview with Ed Koc, Research Director, National Association of Colleges and Employers, 2-13-12). This doesn't mean that graduate students aren't served in this realm. But it is clear that a thirty-five-year-old MBA or twenty-nine-year-old masters in industrial engineering grad student will require a different strategic approach than that of the typical twenty-one-year-old graduating from college. The graduate-level career management issues and development questions differ greatly from those of an undergraduate.

Associations that "Get It" When It Comes to Career Strategy

There are solid examples of associations that "get it" when it comes to providing career-relevant services and activities. The American Society of Association Executives (ASAE) represents one of the best and fully functioning associations in the area of career management. Others include such well-known professional groups as the American Bar Association, Association for Operations Management (APICS), and the American Marketing Association. Many of these (for example, APICS and the American Bar Association) represent professions that have clearly-mapped career progressions marked by education (fundamental and continuing) and certifications. These factors help to make career management, and the association's ability to serve that end, more concrete and noticeable.

Since ASAE is a group of leaders from other associations, I'd like to think that its members promote career management openly and consciously back in the other associations they lead. Look at the benefits ASAE offers in their own association, and how these raise the conversation about career management to a conscious and audible level:

- A career center in operation for ten years
- Mentor—mentee matching service
- Online webinars and in-person career seminars in their Washington DC office
- Low-cost coaching appointments at their annual convention
- Talent development coaching for younger or less experienced directors/executives
- Standard job listings available to members through their website

Unfortunately, the example that ASAE sets seldom carries through to the practices that other associations manifest in their services and programs. But this doesn't prevent you, as a member of any association, from taking initiative. We'll look now at actions you can take within an association to build a more strategic career approach (a solid strategy reaps the benefit of planned action).

Using Your Association Memberships to Better Your Career Advantage

Consider how to take personal responsibility for extracting more value from the time, money, and energy you spend participating in any professional associations. Your approach will depend on a couple of variables:

- Current or upcoming stage of your career
- Which of The Three Career Questions you're trying to answer

Recall in Chapter 3: "When Is It Time to Move Out?," we suggested you start by asking "Who?" and looking to the power and resource of people in your network for deep market intelligence and clues to the current work demands within various organizations. What are associations but people who accumulate knowledge, insight, and influence by banding together? They affiliate around common KISSAs (Knowledge, Interests, Skills, Styles, and Abilities). They add to this a set of shared values and ethics. With all of these in common, it's time to leverage your association membership, along with some additional insights, to find the treasure inside.

Reasons to Join

Let's look at a partial list of some reasons that people join associations. They may wish to gain access to (or insight into):

- Networks;
- Training;
- New practice methods;
- Mentors;
- Free advice;
- Keeping up on trends, regulations, pending legislation;
- Career development services/information;
- Discounts on training, education, and "stuff" (software, computers, tools, books, ammunition);
- Other services—and discounts on those services (insurance, tax services, financial advising, counseling, legal services, etc.).

According to Dalton and Dignam in their 2007 book, *The Decision to Join: How Individuals Determine Value and Why They Choose to Belong* (p. 27), **the nine most common *functions* that a professional association offers are:**

1. Providing training/professional development to members;
2. Providing technical information or professional development to members;
3. Providing timely information about the field to members;
4. Connecting practitioners within the field to each other/networking;
5. Creating and disseminating standards of practice;
6. Representing the field to the public;
7. Representing the field to the government;
8. Representing the field within the industry or discipline;
9. Providing certification opportunities.

The book interprets the responses of a massive survey of sixteen thousand various professional association members and their perceptions about joining, participating, and *leaving* professional associations—and the benefits they desired and derived from them.

Member Rated Top Five Functions of an Association

The members of the survey population ranked the top five (of the total of nine) functions as:

1. Providing training/professional development to members.
2. Providing technical information to members.
3. Providing timely information about the field to members.
4. Connecting practitioners within a field to each other/networking.
5. Creating and disseminating standards of practice.

These all sound pretty good, and probably look like the functions performed by some of the organizations you belong to now, or historically. But HAVING all of those benefits or functions isn't the same as DOING something with them. If you're interested in actively managing your career, it's what you do with these association benefits and functions that really matters. And many people sub-optimize all of those association functions when it comes to career management strategy. They become mere "audience members" at their professional associations—instead of active participants.

If you are dedicated to The Three Career Questions as the core guidance system of your career, and you're monitoring all three at least annually, then there is a good reason to use the resources of the association to help you answer the questions. We have emphasized the need to "think out loud" about The Three Career Questions. Dialogue with trusted others can prevent undue amounts of spin in your own thinking and reduce a phenomenal waste of time and energy. A professional association can be another TOLL (Think Out Loud Laboratory) wherein you can conduct a reality check—expanding or testing your thinking with the input of others who see the marketplace from various angles.

Upon Joining

In Chapter 4 ("When Is It Time to Move Out?"), we talked about the phenomenon of "You're Gone, You're News." As discussed earlier, when you quit or are involuntarily severed from an organization, there is about a six-week window of time where "you're news." Others will want to know your story. When you join a professional organization, as a member of a local chapter, you also have a period of time where you're new—and you're news. **This status of being new is an advantage not to be squandered.**

One of the keys to fruitful participation in an organization is to develop valuable, informative, and well-connected relationships. One thing you can do as a new person in the organization is ask for introductions to senior members who can orient you. Even if your organization has an orientation session for new members, you can still ask specifically for introductions to existing, senior members of the organization. Great conversation topics for your meetings with these senior members might be:

- Trends in the local market, and related topics that the local chapter has focused on over the last year;
- Conferences that the association puts on—regionally, nationally, or even internationally—and the value of attending these major events.

Be sure to attend your association's regional or even national conference. These events represent an enormous efficiency in learning about the profession—as well as insight into the various businesses that support it with services or products. The hottest trends, thinkers, ideas, and methods will be represented by the speakers, vendors, and workshop presenters. The sooner you get up to speed on the major issues and key vocabulary of the association the sooner you'll start to benefit from your membership and the people to whom you'll be introduced.

After Your Newness Wears Off

Ask how you can help. It's important to first get to know the association, or your tribe, and their culture and key leaders before you dive in. This prevents missteps that might make you seem presumptuous or expose your naivety about "how things really work around here." But once you feel you've got the basics down, get involved in the work and leadership of the association.

The people who get the most are typically those who give the most. Giving your time and talent to others forms and deepens relationships. Let's face it, the strongest relationships seem to form with people after you've DONE SOMETHING with them, not just talked or shared ideas.

It takes a lot of different types of work to make a volunteer association run from month to month. I suggest you watch and learn some of the roles that members play while you're in your "newbie phase." When you're ready to step up and help, suggest a role that you feel would best use your talent and fit your time budget and flexibility. Be careful and clear about picking the right volunteer role in an association. There's no better way to sour your relationship with an otherwise solid association than to over-commit to a task or leadership role—and then under-deliver and resent the responsibility.

Mid-Career Members

As you attend conferences—especially the big, annual, national conventions—you may start to notice a phenomenon: **The more experienced members are at the conference, but they aren't attending the workshops and presentations as frequently. They are *presenting* them.**

Being a presenter at a conference is another way to connect to more of your colleagues. You have to carefully decide when you have developed new and meaningful perspectives to offer in the form of a formal presentation. As a caution, be sure you've got something that isn't just a rehash of what others have already known and presented. Once you create that sort of a first impression (as a presenter without a new perspective), it's very hard to un-ring that bell and repair all the first impressions in your audience. But, hopefully you took the advice in Chapter 6 about developing insight:

"A career caution: as information technology increasingly takes over the more simplistic analytical, calculating, and even rational functions of our personal and business decision-making and reasoning, we're left with a new standard of human usefulness and value. It's not what it used to be. It's no longer about having a command over processes. It no longer involves merely controlling information or finding it. Instead, it brings the capacity for insight, creativity, and innovation."

If you've developed that capacity for insight, then you've got some unique thoughts and perspectives—or some experiences and research to offer to others.

Start one year ahead on the process of getting to know the organizers and committee heads so that you will be prepared for the following year's conference. You may want to start persuading them that your topic has current, topical merit before they meet to decide on next year's agenda. But you'll definitely want to get on the list of potential speakers who will receive the request for proposals (RFPs) to speak at the next conference.

The other phenomenon that you may notice is that the more experienced members are using the conferences less for education and more for connecting with others. The other reason they aren't in the workshops is that they are meeting with colleagues, customers, clients, and prospects who have all conveniently gathered at this one time and place. This gives them an enormous opportunity to do business on a face-to-face basis. Their schedules are filled with mini-meetings, cocktail receptions, and lunch or dinner tables that may be reserved for a select membership group. As business communications becomes more electronic and virtual— and as travel budgets contract—the reduced number of opportunities to meet in person makes each outing increasingly valuable.

Local, regional, and national meetings are your chance to get the "chemistry" right between you and key others with whom you will do business or research. We are still, undeniably, organic beings who perceive important things about each other from the interpersonal interactions that happen in real-time, close quarters. Miscalculate that reality, and you may find that your obsession with the speed and convenience of email also finds you in the middle of professional relationships wherein you are viewed as nothing more than an effective conduit for information. Instead, you want to be seen as a trusted, personally-known source of insight, thought, and advice.

Senior Membership and Mentoring

Experienced members of your association represent a source of mentors and guides. Look for mentors in professional associations, especially if you work in a particularly small or start-up type of organization. Your workplace may not have the quality, experience level, or right chemistry for you to feel comfortable relating to someone as a mentor. The professional association can act as an extension of your work culture—providing you with relevant sources of mentoring.

Mentors are distinguished from coaches and consultants in that they are valued as experts in their career paths—not necessarily because of their content knowledge or techniques. Their ability to patiently hear others' career stories and tell their own is extremely valuable. The mentor's story comes complete with insights as to the good and bad moves made during their careers. This makes them uniquely able to contribute valuable 20/20 hindsight. Technical advisors or counselors may not have such hindsight.

The role of mentor may be a valuable contribution that only experienced, senior members of a professional association can make. In the last stage of one's career, the spirit of *generativity* becomes strong and real for many.

Key Term

Generativity is the natural tendency to want to create or nurture that which will survive you in an organization—or in the culture as a whole.

Generativity involves mentoring the next group of leaders who are coming behind you—so that they can advance, perhaps bringing your legacy or accomplishments with them. It may mean leaving an endowment or strong balance sheet for an association to carry on its work. It may mean attending meetings in a non-leadership role just to be that blessedly available, experienced person who can fill any role needed when a critical player is absent.

How The Three Career Questions Play Out in Associations

Let's look at some specific ways to leverage your association participation in the framework of The Three Career Questions.

Time to Move Up?

- **You may want to find a mentor who is outside your organization.** Let's face it. There are political dynamics and loyalties inside your organization. These can cause your mentor to be less than candid if doing so might jeopardize:
  - Confidentiality;
  - A relationship with someone else;
  - The retention of you.

    Hearing about the path of a senior professional—who works somewhere else and can be completely open about the good, the bad, and the ugly—can be most instructive and certainly more entertaining.

- **See and talk with living examples of what it might look like to progress within an area of work.** How satisfied and happy do senior members of the profession appear to be? Are they living a version of "success" that suits you (Chapter 5: "Success: If Only We Knew What That Was?")

- **Get a preview.** Be able to discuss leadership responsibilities and skills before you take on your first management role or accept a major jump in responsibility level. Hear from others about some of the landmines before you step on them.

- **Learn from others about some of the key lessons learned and experiences you might want to include in your learning plan.**
- **Access professional education, training, and development resources through the association.** This could include scholarships or grants to enhance your level of education. It also could include funds to further develop your place of work—such as a lab or classroom (for example, check out the Association of American Educators' Teacher Scholarships & Classroom Grants at AAETeachers.org).
- **Observe and adopt the dress, vocabulary, and content knowledge of the next professional level or tribe you want to join.** Let's say you've worked in a super casual environment within corporate finance at Nike for eight years, and you just accepted a role in international banking in New York. A professional association's national conference would be a great way to check out the customs and style of your future tribe before landing in the mid-town Manhattan in khakis and cross-trainers.

When It's Time to Move Out

- Career Centers, job search groups, job listings, and career consultants are actual support services offered by some professional associations (such as Financial Executives International [FEI] and Financial Executives Networking Group [FENG], its sister organization for professionals in career transition). This is the time to take advantage of them. Your membership dues have been paying for them.
- If you're contemplating a move in a year or two, now is the time to start consciously reinforcing and diversifying your network of professional contacts. Depending on how confidential you need to be, the national or regional conferences

may be better places to explore than within your small, local association chapter events.

- Your professional association is a readily available cross-section of the profession and can help you prevent a false-positive move. People frequently "Move Out" of their jobs as a quick-and-dirty way to resolve a problematic work situation or collegial relationship.

Take, for example, the former non-profit medical relief worker who goes to work at an urban, managed healthcare provider and feels oppressed and constrained by all the cost-containment restrictions on his work. He may quit, only to subsequently discover that nearly all of the other healthcare organizations he explores have essentially the same culture and potential to disappoint him. He should have been asking, "When is it time to Adapt My Style for greater success?"

Use the association's cross-section of members as a place to survey the market before you make any major decisions or moves. Have some crucial conversations among your professional association members who can compare organizational cultural attributes and business models. They may help you see if you're in the wrong industry or profession, rather than just the wrong organization.

If you're listening to the trends and topics being discussed within your association's conferences and professional development seminars, you'll start to pick up trends. Are these trends pointing toward growth, consolidation, constriction, and/or international (versus domestic) expansion? These seminars and conferences can offer clues as to whether your profession or industry is about to head in a direction that does or does not coincide with your values or development plans.

In Chapter 4 ("When Is It Time to Move Out?"), we said it

starts by asking, "Who?" The people who know about your target market and organizations you might want to work for are nicely concentrated into professional associations. They will help you research your opportunities and develop your Focus Of Inquiry into target markets and places where the work lurks before it has even been declared a j-o-b. This is crowd sourcing at its intimate best.

Look also at the marketplace challenges that professional associations address in their programs. These challenges are mentioned on page 28 in *The Decision to Join: How Individuals Determine Value and Why They Choose to Belong*, by James Dalton and Monica Dignam (2007). Their list of challenges demonstrates the outward focus that the association shares with you as an individual. Issues such as quality, technology advancements, and professional recognition in the market are all examples of matters that eventually impact you personally. These are the challenges that associations are trying to address on behalf of you, the member. The challenges listed below are representative of the very problems, issues, needs, and trends that will be part of your Focus Of Inquiry as you prepare to look for new work in any sector of our economy. Take a good look.

16 Challenges That Face Professional Communities

(Not the association itself but the community of workers that it represents.)

1. Inadequate recognition of the value delivered by the profession or discipline to the larger society
2. Keeping up with new information in the field
3. Lack of public awareness of your field
4. Inadequate sources of funding or revenue
5. Keeping pace with technology
6. An expanding body of knowledge

7. Challenging regulatory environment (needed relief from regulations)
8. Inadequate supply of capable professionals
9. Cost
10. Achieving high-quality outcomes
11. Increasing competition (domestic or international)
12. Rapidly changing, difficult
13. Liability exposure, risk management
14. Inadequate supply of support personnel
15. Undesirable pending legislation
16. Technology replacing practitioners

Refine any of these sixteen challenges into questions you can ask about your industry, and you'll be able to pursue valuable, networking-driven, market research with networking partners. Your exploration of these challenges through conversations in the marketplace will lead you to:

- Formulate basic understandings of the hot spots in the profession;
- Decide what sounds interesting to you and where your experience can make the biggest impact;
- Design astute questions to ask during your network-driven research so as to become better informed at the level of an industry insider;
- Gather information to offer during networking exchanges regarding solutions, innovations, resources, and positioning ideas (SIRP) for the problems, issues, needs, and trends (PINT) you're researching.

When It's Time to Adapt Your Style

Answering the question of when to Adapt Your Style may be a bit harder through your participation in a professional association. Let's face it; we're all on our best behavior and "lookin' good" when we attend events outside our place of work. Consequently, our colleagues and fellow association members are less likely to see aspects of our technical expertise or management style that we need to improve or modify. For this reason, we may suffer from unduly or naively supportive colleagues who see only positive styles and therefore constantly reassure us or minimize our concerns about our work.

Board and Committee Work. Board or committee work in your association may be the best way to gain safe and realistic feedback. If you've had the opportunity to work on committees or boards within an association, others working with you will have had a chance to observe something closer to your leadership style and ability to get work done. Harness their observations and perceptions.

Let them know of your interest in answering the third question: when is it time to Adapt My Style? And be open about your need for some candid feedback. Be ready to hear feedback that is critical or at least not as positive as you might have hoped. Reassure people that you appreciate the information as part of your effort to gather and understand *perceptions*. Feedback from colleagues on the board or committee mimics the feedback that you really need to get from people at work. Remember from Chapter 3 ("When Is It Time to Move Up?"), it's your responsibility to create a feedback-rich environment for yourself. Professional associations, and your colleagues there, may offer as ripe an opportunity for viable feedback and coaching as your workplace.

Professional Competency Models. Professional standards and competency models are one of the other resources generated by professional associations. These models and standards can be invaluable for doing your own assessment of where you stand in the profession and, by implication, where you may stand in your work organization. These competency models offer good places to start an honest self-assessment of your professional skills and style.

We're all familiar with standards and ethics set by such organizations as the American Medical Association and the American Bar Association. But dig a little, and you'll find competency models for people in other professions—such as the training and development field. Within the archives of the American Society for Training and Development (ASTD.org), you can find a competency model that clearly indicates the range and depth of what members of this profession need to know about the profession's different roles.

If you're new to a field, or have for developmental purposes switched to a new functional area of business (such as from safety and facilities to training and development), this is a quick way to see how much you need to learn and how much you may need to adapt your former style of leadership or interpersonal interactions.

In addition, the Institute of Management Consultants (IMCUSA.org) has both a competency model for consulting as well as a code of ethics. These strongly characterize what they stand for and the STYLE with which they ask all members to practice. As a meeting participant at an IMCUSA event, you can feel the tension in the room when new members or visitors tell stories about how they conduct business, and the style they're exhibiting or describing is living proof that they've not yet read the code of ethics.

Mentor/Advisor/Guide/Role Model. Last but not least, in a professional association, you have the chance to find experienced, professional, and successful members who may have made a transition similar to yours—or one that you're contemplating. They may have struggled with moves into the professions or organizations they wanted to work for. If their struggles precede you by a few years, they may offer some perspective, lessons learned, and suggestions that could be very helpful. Think about shopping for such a just-in-time, mini-mentor by scrutinizing the list of presenters at a professional conference. The clues offered in a speaker's bio or workshop description would help you find a mentor/advisor who could focus your search and make it more efficient. More experienced association members on the board of directors may be quite complimented by your request for some insights about their pathways into or around the professions and inside their current organizations. In the spirit of great network-ing, don't forget to ask them for their introductions to other asso-ciation members who have encountered the same hurdle you're trying to get over. Keep your network growing through a focused inquiry and thoughtful conversations with experienced members of your professional association.

Closing Thoughts

What we have portrayed in *Answering The Three Career Questions: Your Lifetime Career Management System* is the range of thinking, questioning, and actions necessary to bring someone like you to the point of:

- Acknowledging your intuitions about your work and the need for change;
- Clarifying the appropriate career question to be answering at this time in your life and in the future;
- Providing some methods and tools that help you answer that right question and pursue the answers as part of an action strategy, not just an intellectual awareness.

The Problem

- People keep getting *one job in a row,* and they feel like they're not succeeding. **They need a bigger theory of the game; think *career management*.**
- Most of us will change jobs more than a dozen times and likely have a few career changes along the way too. Without a career management strategy, a lot of these changes will be done **to** you, not **by** you.

Solution

- Answer The Three Career Questions continuously throughout your work life, and manage your career for greater personal success.
- The Three Career Questions system gets you "career management," not "serial job-finding." You'll be able to create career strategy—and reap the advantages of planned actions.

Why 3?

- Each time your job crashed, the *"Parachute"* book helped you take off again and land a new job. *The Three Career Questions* book and career management system keep you aloft in the first place and help you reduce the number of *unscheduled landings* you'll have to endure and recover from throughout your working years. *The Three Career Questions* completes your *flight operations manual* for career management success. Now, you can stay aloft longer and make the moves you choose, not the ones dictated by the rapidly approaching ground.

I hope you use this book to the benefit of your own work and the downstream benefit of all your future colleagues, customers, clients, and patients. As many career consultants have found, some clients can read books like this and really take off on their own—changing the way they more productively manage their careers. Others may understand all the words, but not know how to implement what they are reading. And still others may not "get" this new way of thinking about managing their careers. The latter group most likely needs time in the Think Out Loud Laboratory with trusted colleagues or career consultants to dialogue their way through The Three Career Questions.

Unfortunately, circumstances will manage careers in strange sorts of ways. If you exert very little personal initiative and remain passive regarding your career, events will happen to you that resemble a career. You may not, however, love what the result looks like. **If you take a Career Self-Reliant approach to more actively manage your career for intentional (but not guaranteed) outcomes, you'll feel the difference. You'll like the outcomes and the feeling of being more in charge of co-creating your results.** An indecisive, motionless, inactive talent in our work culture is a victim waiting to happen. Instead of that, keep your knees bent and *imagine that you can choose to constantly be ready to Move Up, Move Out, or Adapt Your Style.*

Want More?

Visit www.3questionsconsulting.com to purchase and download an extra PDF set of the questionnaires and tools from this book to use for yourself—or to offer to friends and colleagues as they answer The Three Career Questions.

ABOUT THE AUTHOR

Bruce Blackstone Hazen,
Three Questions Consulting

Bruce Hazen is a highly-respected speaker, consultant, coach, and author who specializes in helping individual and corporate clients navigate change, manage careers, and mentor others utilizing his "The Three Career Questions" system. The system has been developed and road-tested over years of working with individuals as well as business and non-profit organizations that are eager to leverage The Three Career Questions system as a way to accelerate and focus their talent management strategy when it's time to:

- **Move up?**

  Development planning to create progression at every level

- **Move out?**

  Redeployment and exit plans that strive for win-win quality

- **Adapt styles?**

  Leader coaching to define and "behavioralize" (not intellectualize) success

Mr. Hazen's own career, training, and experiences represent a managed process that has:

- Built on previous lessons and experiences;
- Diversified skills and perceptions;
- Stayed professionally and geographically flexible.

He thus serves as a contemporary example of career development and the shift from a "job" mentality to an emphasis on fulfilling the *work* that is needed by organizational clients, communities, and individuals. His first-hand experience with his consulting model enables him to speak of and demonstrate principles important to the field of career management, organizational leadership, and the process of change and transition in leadership coaching.

Current Work

As a career and management consultant, Bruce combines business systems experience with clinical understanding to address the needs of individuals in a range of different professions who are managing other people, organizations, and their own career development. He is the President of Three Questions Consulting in Portland, Oregon, where he lives with his wife Jennifer and Emi, the most adorable rescued Shiba Inu dog.

Experience

Bruce has extensive and diverse industry experience as an internal and external consultant, and member of corporate staff and line management. Arenas of work have included electronics design and manufacturing, financial services, footwear/apparel, e-business, utilities, health care, legal, education, community services, international civil engineering, and global outplacement.

His work with managing change and transition began with Fluor Corporation while acting as the Director of Employee Assistance. Subsequently, as Director of the largest Employee Assistance Program in the American public education, he managed the delivery of services to 37,000 employees of the L.A. Unified School District. While a member of regional management for a health care company, he successfully helped manage the merger of three companies into one of the first managed healthcare companies on the West Coast.

Staffing, recruiting, career and management development, learning services, outplacement, and organization development services are areas of professional accomplishment. He has delivered service on an internal and external consulting basis within such organizations as Tektronix, Adidas America, Nike, Hewlett

Packard, Wells Fargo Bank, PacifiCorp, and the Federal Reserve Bank of Boston. Clients have ranged from startups with five employees to companies of more than 100,000. Bruce has held both staff and management positions within the health care industry and human resources field.

Education and Affiliation

Bruce has a B.S. in Industrial and Labor Relations from Cornell University with emphasis in organizational behavior and psychology. In addition, he holds a Masters Degree of Science in Clinical Psychology from California State University, San Jose, and is active within the Institute of Management Consultants (IMC), the American Society for Training and Development (ASTD), and the Oregon Career Development Association (ODCN).

For more on Bruce's consulting, or to contact him directly, please visit www.ThreeQuestionsConsulting.com, or bruce@ threequestionsconsulting.com.

SOURCES

Preface

Sears, S. (1982), "A Definition of Career Guidance Terms: A National Vocational Guidance Association Perspective." *Vocational Guidance Quarterly*, 31: 137–143.

Chapter 2

Drake, David B. (2007). "The art of thinking narratively: Implications for coaching psychology and practice." *Australian Psychologist*, 42(4), 283–294

Fisher, W.R. *Human Communication as a Narration: Toward a Philosophy of Reason, Value, and Action.* Columbia, SC: University of South Carolina Press. 1987.

Holland, John L. *Making Vocational Choices: A Theory of Vocational Personalities and Work Environments* (3rd Ed.). Odessa, FL: Psychological Assessment Resources. 1997.

Ibarra, H. *Working Identity: Unconventional Strategies for Reinventing Your Career.* Boston: Harvard Business School Press. 2004.

Chapter 3

Maslow, A. Motivation and Personality *(2nd Ed.). New York: Harper & Row. 1970.*

Center for Creative Leadership, Greensboro, North Carolina. Leadership research that was the foundation for the Benchmarks assessment tool described in:

- McCall, Morgan Jr., Lombardo, Michael M., and Morrison, Ann M. *The Lessons of Experience: How Successful Executives Develop on the Job.* Landham, MD: Lexington Books. 1988.
- Leslie, Jean Brittain, and Van Velsor, Ellen. *A Look at Derailment Today: North America and Europe.* Greensboro, NC: CCL Press. 1996.

Chapter 4

Tichy, Noel. *Organizational Dynamics*. Maryland Heights, MO: Elsevier. 1982.

Farren, Caela, PhD. *Who's Running Your Career? Creating Stable Work in Unstable Times*. Austin, TX: Bard Press. 1987.

Chapter 5

Blanchard, Ken. *Leadership and the One-Minute Manager: Increasing Effectiveness Through Situational Leadership*. New York: William Morrow. 1999.

Chapter 6

Career Action Center. "Self-Reliance is the New Reality of Work, Competition, Companies and Life," edited transcript of speech by Scott Cook, at the 14th annual Pinnacle Luncheon, sponsored by the Career Action Center. 1996.

Collard, Betsy A., Epperheimer, John W., & Saign, Diane. "Career Resilience in a Changing Workplace." (See http://www.eric.ed.gov/PDFS/ED396191.pdf) Adapted from information *Series No. 366, ERIC Clearinghouse on Adult, Career and Vocational Education Center on Education and Training for Employment*. 1996.

Chapter 7

Dalton, James, and Dignam, Monica. *The Decision to Join: How Individuals Determine Value and Why They Choose to Belong*. Washington DC: Association Management Press. 2007.

Want More?

Visit www.3questionsconsulting.com to download an extra PDF set of the questionnaires and tools from this book to use for yourself—or to offer to friends and colleagues as they answer The Three Career Questions. See an example of an individual's completed set of questionnaires and the development plan that resulted from the insights he gained.